"WHY MY SON?"

"WHY MY SON?"

A Dad's Struggle To Find Peace

CHRIS BREEN

authorHOUSE®

AuthorHouse™
1663 Liberty Drive
Bloomington, IN 47403
www.authorhouse.com
Phone: 1-800-839-8640

Published by AuthorHouse 04/13/2013

ISBN: 978-1-4772-4053-3 (sc)
ISBN: 978-1-4772-4052-6 (e)

Library of Congress Control Number: 2012912046

This book is printed on acid-free paper.

Dedication

I dedicate this book to my Son Nathaniel, whose life has not turned out the way he wanted it to be, who unknowingly touches the lives around him. You are my buddy, I am your dad. I Love You!

CHAPTER I

"What The Hell Is Happening Here?"

When my wife to be, Kimberly and myself prepared to get married in June of 1998, we had the same hopes and dreams every couple have; getting married to the one you love, having children, raising a family and then live the rest of our lives together in each other's arms knowing we did our very best for our children and ourselves. This plan will have its ups and downs, but if you do it just right and work together, when you get to that part of retiring and you are playing with your grandchildren (possibly great-grandchildren) at the beach on your permanent vacation, life would have been so enjoyable.

Well something happened early on in our journey so we can throw that plan right out the metaphoric window. His name is Nathaniel, My only son. He is the middle of our three children (Courtney is two years older and Emma is two years younger). At birth Nathaniel sustained a severe brain injury which later was diagnosed as Cerebral Palsy. He also has a seizure disorder, cortical blindness, scoliosis and is on a bevy of medications (some every day, some as needed) to keep him as balanced as possible. Nathaniel and his family have been on a roller coaster ride to the brink and back many a time and you know what, no one understands us. No one understands why I am late for work or why Kim spends a good bit of her waking day on the phone keeping Nathaniel's entities in line all the while getting Courtney and Emma motivated for the day ahead of them.

This book represents Nathaniel's life challenges and the day to day activities of a family with a child who has a disability. This book also represents the legions of families across the globe that are in our shoes.

(February 19, 2001)

(Kim is home, but Nathaniel is still in the hospital. The doctors are talking about him having his seizures. His arms straighten out, a little to the left for maybe fifteen to twenty seconds at least three or four times an hour. We cannot hold or even touch him. The nurse keeps telling us we can cause a seizure if we touch him. All I see are a lot of wires and tubes. They say we may be able to hold Nathaniel today for the first time and that he may be able to come home in a few days. They also say a lot of things that I do not understand. I don't know if we can do this. No one has told us what to do or what to expect. I am scared for Nathaniel. Kim must be scared too, but she does not show it. Courtney is so excited.)

The main purpose in life as a father is to be the caretaker and protector of his family. Your wife and children are the single most important features in a father's life. When you do not have control over something concerning a family member, you are rendered helpless. You want answers to every question you ask, and you want everything to be corrected sooner rather than later. As the world seems to be crashing down around me, I asked out loud "What the hell is happening here?" Of course I was escorted out of the N.I.C.U. (Neonatal Intensive Care Unit) to calm down and given no answers. Listen, I have learned to deal with things when it happens to me, but when it happened to my new born son, the level of helplessness went through the roof.

It happened to my dearest and only son Nathaniel, and I was helpless. It was Valentine's Day 2001, only two days before his due date. So I thought, "This is going to be great, the birth of my son or daughter on the day to celebrate love." But it turned out to be a day of horror. Now you may say "Isn't "horror" a bit harsh?" I say no! I say it was the day I lost my faith. My son's life was changed forever. Kim motherly intuition kicked in and knew something was not going well. Nathaniel was in distress and an emergency C-section was performed and the problems started mounting. So how would you feel if your child was born and you were "demanded" not to touch him because "You" could set him off into a seizure. Or a year later you were told that three-quarters of your son's brain is damaged and basically dormant of brainwaves. How would you react?

There are some of us out here that have heard these words or even something worse. Believe it or not, some have totally walked away from this situation, abandoning their children. Couples have even divorced over things like this because they don't want it (referring to their son or daughter). As broken hearted as Kim and I were, we bonded even more. There are legions of families in this world who are heartbroken and in the same boat as us, but we have to be determined to work harder than you can possibly imagine.

As you read on, the majority of my writing comes from time I wish I did not have. The words you are reading now and I can honestly say one half of this book was written while I am in the hospital with Nathaniel. A trip to the emergency room or a hospital stay has a lot of down time, and when it is just Nathaniel and myself I like to write when he is resting. It is quiet and a lot of thoughts run through my head at these times. So I figured, "let's document our time." So let me introduce myself, I am Chris Breen, the husband of Kimberly and the father of three (Courtney, Nathaniel and Emma). I am a simple man; I try to go with the flow. I am nowhere near perfect (except that one time I threw a no-hitter back in little league). Look, I try to joke a lot; I guess it is my way of trying to cope out loud with Nathaniel's disability. I will never try to hide behind that part of his life. He is hurt and he needs me. Also, I have never really talked to anyone about what has happened to him. No psychiatrist, therapist, priest or anyone. I guess you can say this book is my release or therapy.

As you read this book I am pouring out my broken heart onto these pages. Reflecting back on everything hurts so badly. There are times I just have to walk away and regroup my thoughts. I just want people to know my son, our plight and what many families go through around our world. Kim and I live paycheck to paycheck and struggle mightily at times to get through the month just to do it all over again the following month. Listen, we have two beautiful daughters that deserve the "American Dream" just like everyone else.

Now a days the "American Dream" is a bit distorted, so I will just say a comfortable life where in which when they grow up they have an education and smart head on their shoulders.

When I was growing up in Broomall, PA (a suburb of Philadelphia), I had a very normal life. Did the basics, went to school, which I struggled with at times, I was a sports freak (hockey and baseball) and I kept my life clean. Yeah, I made my share of mistakes, but who didn't? I was the youngest of eight kids, known as the spoiled one. My dad, Jim past away when I was in the fourth grade and I was raised by my mom, Catherine, grand mom Sarah, Aunt Pat, and my cousin Anna all in one house. Because of growing up around these beautiful and knowledgeable women I feel I am more in touch with my emotions and feelings. I knew I wanted to get married and have children. As I realized this I would sometimes imagine myself as a husband and a father. And a couple of times I would think, "What if I had a sick child or my wife would get sick and I would have to take care of them? I would play it over and over in my mind. As I think back on it I use to say to myself, "Deal with it!" So, unfortunately it did come true to both my son and wife, and I still am learning day to day, but I learned you deal with whatever comes your way. It is one of the hardest things to learn and endure. There was that period of being scared for Nathaniel, and then I would say; "What the hell is happening here?", and then it was rage. And I am talking about full-blown, off-the-wall rage. And do not forget with all of this swirling I have a two year old daughter who needs her dad. Courtney being born first was a blessing in disguise because she was my calm in the eye of the storm. She kept Kim and I focused as parents. The one explicit memory I have with Courtney was a few days after Nathaniel was born. On my ride home from the hospital I felt my anger starting to build up, and this helpless feeling came over me. I cried all the way home. I had to put it in the back of my mind and focus on Courtney. So we get in the house and had some dinner, had a bubble bath and did our normal rituals before bed time. Courtney wanted to play a little before bed. I figured this will be great for her, she was back and forth so much from home to the hospital since Nathaniel was born; she needed this time. We had just bought a new thirty six inch daddy dream TV. So I kept the huge box for Courtney to play in. I cut out a door and a couple of windows and soon she was in her own little world. And you know what, so was I. I am a big guy so I could not fit in her house when I was invited over for some tea. So I laid 1/3 in the house and 2/3 out. For the next hour life was simple and the most pleasurable I have ever had as a father. This hour was a father's dream come true in the middle of an absolute nightmare.

(March 5, 2001)

(I am at work. Nathaniel has been home for almost two weeks now, but this is crazy. We went to see Nathaniel's regular pediatric doctor and she says he is pretty healthy for what he is going through. He cries a lot. Sometimes it feels like there is no way to console him. We also saw a neurologist at the University of Delaware. No, DuPont Children's Hospital in Delaware. I don't even know where I am because of the lack of sleep. No one is saying exactly what is going on, like something happened but nobody wants to say or diagnose what is happening.)

(March 19, 2001)

(This is nuts! Our sanity is being tested. Nathaniel cries practically the whole time he is awake. The doctors want him to have a seizure medication called Phenobarbital. We have to give it to him, but it makes him choke. Peppermint flavored and very strong. Now we are told to give it to him with one ounce of formula then give him his regular bottle. But it takes him forever to drink his bottle, like he forgets what he is doing.)

There I go again using words not usually in my vocabulary. This was to be the day of the birth of a beautiful child. These are the days that live with you forever. We did not get the respect needed at the time. Hey, look, since Nathaniel's birth I have met some of the most passionate doctors and nurses who are sometimes so blunt and to the point. As much as I may not want to hear what is being said, for once it has been the truth. It hurts, but it helps you realize what we are up against.

With everything that was going on, I started to realize the real trouble brewing when we were taking Nathaniel home for the first time. No one told us what to do or what to expect. Man, they could not even look us in the face. So there we were with no information about his seizures or about his constant crying, just go home and make an appointment with a neurologist at DuPont Children's Hospital in Delaware. Not even a sorry. How could you not look into a mother's or father's eyes when things are not right. I do believe the human spirit could not let you do that day after day, or even once. In our case, we were two days before our due date with not one complication with the entire pregnancy. Three words that I just can't stand since that day are "Act of God". All of what has happened was due to an "Act of God". Growing up Catholic, I was always taught God does not act like that.

Listen, I am no expert, nor is Kim, we were just as scared for Nathaniel's life as every other person that day, and the only thing I needed was respect. I was treated like I had no clue what was going on. And you know what, they were right; I did not know anything, but a little talking to as an adult not a child with his hand in the cookie jar just before dinner would have been appreciated. We were made to feel as low as a human being could be. We were given updates after the birth but they were sketchy at best. The frustration level was at an all-time high. I just wanted to see my boy. If only for a moment, I just wanted to see him. Hold his fingers; let him know daddy was right there beside him. I thought maybe if he heard my voice it could help him. Instead, the next sentence I hear set me off. A nurse, who I asked to see repeatedly for hours, finally came to get us to see Nathaniel. I went by myself first because Kim was still unable to get up after her emergency C-section. So I met the nurse at the prep room before entering the N.I.C.U. (For those of you who have never experienced an N.I.C.U., be thankful. Do not get me wrong, there is hope in this unit, too. For what I experienced, I wish it on no one.)

The first words out of this nurse's mouth were "You are the father of . . . ?" That was it. There I go again thinking, "What the hell is happening here?" This nurse, eight hours after Nathaniel's birth, should know who the parents are, you'd think? So I tried to focus on Nathaniel. When entering the N.I.C.U. you must scrub your hands and arms just like a surgeon does before entering to operating room. A mask and gown for now also. The second I entered there were two sounds I will never forget for as long as I live. They were the ventilators on the children and the beeping of the monitors. It was an unsettling feeling.

So here I finally was, seeing my son for the very first time. Of course, I was excited to introduce myself to him, but at the same time, I was apprehensive. I did not know what to expect, but as I walked closer, my heart sank. A ventilator tube down his throat, wires around his fingers, forearms and legs. An IV line in the side of Nathaniel's head (they had a hard time finding some veins). Monitors, everywhere. I could barely see his face. He looked so frail, vulnerable to the world that awaits him. I remember it as if it were yesterday. His closed eyes twitching, body very jumpy, as if he were having a bad dream.

I held my composure as best I could. I felt sorry, almost guilty. I knew right then and there I have to be strong for him, Courtney and Kim. So I talked to him gently. Letting him know I was right by his side and mommy and Courtney could not wait to see him. I kissed my fingers, reached out to touch his forehead and the nurse startled me by demanding me not to touch him because I may set him off into a seizure. A seizure? How? Why? I asked. She said for now the doctors and nurses are the only ones who could touch him. I felt even worse than before. And you know what, I still have not been told what happened, why it happened and what is going on now. So I asked to talk to his doctor. I sat with Nathaniel for about 20 minutes until the doctor finally came over to talk with me. This is the part I have been waiting for. Just like those lives in the ER or hospital dramas that the doctor takes aside a loved one and explains from A to Z what has happened since the arrival of Nathaniel in the hospital.

He explained with all generic answers. "Your son had problems at birth." No shit!

Then he said, "He is still sick now." You think! And that "We are monitoring him around the clock." No matter whom you asked the same answers came out of their mouths. At the same time of the birth of a child when things go wrong, I guess there are no exact answers for what is happening so early on, but this felt different. We felt that something went wrong after we finally meeting Nathaniel for the first time. I was heading back to Kim's room and I was completely numb. I walked down the hall to the elevator. I don't remember if I acknowledged anyone or if anyone was there at all. I went straight to Kim's room. At this point Kim still has not seen Nathaniel, so when I walked in her room Kim had an excited but worried look about her. I broke down in her arms immediately. I remember telling Kim about the tubes and wires and how helpless I felt. I said over and over "This is serious, what has happened to him?" I was never so scared for some one's life besides my own.

Kim proceeds to tell me that the doctor who actually saved Nathaniel's life when he performed an emergency C-section after six hours of waiting in her hospital room (yes, I did say six hours of waiting to see the doctor on call) came by to check on Kim. He said he was sorry for what went on and sorry it took so long to get something done. He sat and cried with

Kim for a moment and he had to leave just before I came back. Since then this doctor has passed on, and for what it's worth, I do thank him. That moment Kim did share, that was it. My son is fighting for his life one floor above us and we are left to wonder what went wrong. This is the first time I realized I should keep a journal of what is going on and why. Then I start to think how things could go so wrong so fast. Kim and I enjoy the family life. We enjoy watching Courtney figure out our world. We enjoy the company of family and friends, and how we teach and learn from each other the ways to take care of our children, you know, learn those home remedies to take care of a sick child. We take and give advice to other parents and find our way to deal. Now our world is crashing down around us. You can try to say to yourself and your wife everything is going to be fine, but I know from the moment I saw Nathaniel, our lives were about to change drastically and it scared the hell out of me. Why is this happening to Nathaniel? Why him? Why us? He did nothing wrong. He was doing what he was supposed to be doing. Why did no one pay attention to Kimberly? The reactions (no matter how much Kim pressed the issue) she got from the Nurses were like "It's not that bad" and "This is normal." No one took her seriously. Damn it!

Friends and family came to visit bringing balloons with "It's a Boy!" on them. Nathaniel gets outstanding presents of Philadelphia Flyers and Eagles outfits. But the mood was different, and difficult. I felt robbed and cheated. My son has not even met his mommy yet. How scared do you think Nathaniel feels? I don't even know if he is scared. He may be brain damaged. What is he feeling? What is he hearing? You cannot even hear him cry out because of the tube down his throat. I wonder, "Does he want to hear my voice again to assure him everything is OK?"

So much shit is running through my mind. So many things being talked about that I don't understand. The doctors and nurses talking in medical lingo. And the only thing I want is to hold my son. I thought it could do a world of good, but not now for he is sick enough that a touch could set him off into a seizure. That I can accept. I do not want to hurt him or cause him pain. What were hard to accept were witnessing Nathaniel's seizures. I was 31 years old and I never had physically seen a seizure except for what I saw on TV. Witnessing my first seizure was hard to swallow; it literally scared the shit out of me. Nathaniel, while lying on his back, he would extend his arms up in the air, stiff and angled to the left. His closed eyes would shutter, as if he was blinking with his eyes closed. My heart wept. I felt as low as a human can possible go. What made things worse for me was witnessing the second seizure 20 minutes later. I suddenly excused myself, walked out into the hall bathroom and threw my guts up. The pit of my stomach ached for hours, come to think of it, that ache is still there today. On the other hand, maybe it was me losing my faith in God. Asking why, over and over. I found myself next heading to the hospital chapel praying for my son's life, then all of the sudden here I was yelling at my God for letting this travesty to take place. Then I threw up again right there on the chapel floor. This God-awful harsh feeling in the pit of my stomach took control of me. I was full of rage. I remember saying "why him? Why Nathaniel? What did he do to you? He is innocent!" I cursed my God to no end. Growing up as a Catholic, even as an altar boy at my church, I thought I should have bursted into flames right there in that chapel. I said this with one eye peering back over my shoulder. I was scared, but so mad. Here I am standing up to my God as if he was some bully beating up on a weaker kid. I was not going to let him do this to my child. I challenged him, demanding him to put me in Nathaniel's place. I fell to the floor, weakened by my anguish as if I were beaten down also. There was a dead calm in the room, the kind of calm and quiet I had a ringing in my ears.

I don't know, maybe five or ten minutes went by and I picked myself off the floor, scrubbed my hands and arms, walked back into the N.I.C.U. and continued my vigil with Nathaniel. I have to be there for him, Courtney and Kim, and Emma later on. There has to be a way to go forward.

With all of this hectic and crazy moments going on we still do not know what will happen with Nathaniel. I thought early on that this may only be temporary and he will get better and be a normal child. But as time moved on in the hospital, I realized the damage may have already been done. My mom, who is a Charismatic Catholic, said to me, "He will be OK, leave it in God's hands to take care of Nathaniel." For the first time in my life, I said to my mom, "To hell with God, if there is one!" If there was one thing NOT to say to my mom, those were the eight words. It was one of those burst into flames moments again, but she saw that I had lost my way, my faith. I said to her, "If God is so great and loving, why is he doing this to an innocent child." "Nathaniel is innocent!" "Why him?" She saw a broken son. I stood up to my God and my mom in a 24 hour period. I was wrecked.

But again, I have to be strong. My family needs me. I was torn. I was strong to keep the values of love of family and one another through God to keep moving, and then I felt this emptiness that God let Nathaniel down at birth. My emotions were playing with me. I look at Courtney at the window of the N.I.C.U. looking to get a peek at her new brother, and I think of the innocence of childhood and her curiosity of meeting her brother for the first time. Then I look at Nathaniel and I actually thought one time and ONLY ONE TIME, "Damaged goods!" I hated myself forever thinking those words. I could be at work, home or wherever and at any moment I would feel sorrow, rage, joy and happiness all within a ten minute span. I would find myself some days in the back of a church asking for forgiveness and guidance. I guess this is my test in life. Growing up I was taught that as we go through life we will be tested and tempted. Well, this is one hell of a test and this is my testimonial. I do not stand up to my God anymore and I have asked him for forgiveness since then. I still have some Christian values and I do pray every day for my family and my friends. And even for the people who wronged Nathaniel. I told my mom I was sorry for what I said about God, and of course, she smiled at me and said, "It's OK God still and always love you." (My mom passed away on July 2, 2007, and I know she guides my hand as I pour my thoughts and feelings on these pages. I miss you mom, watch over us.)

When it came time to bring Nathaniel home, our frustration level went way up. We were only told to set an appointment with Nathaniel's pediatrician and find a neurologist. It was wonderful bringing Nathaniel home, but I sense from Kim's apprehension, and I feel it too.

I set Nathaniel down in his car seat carrier on the living room floor. He was sleeping quietly. But I felt our stormy future brewing all around us. So for now we wait. Wait for what? Answers? The truth? Apologies? Yeah, right! I feel helpless, almost guilty. Is there something I could have done to have changed our situation? What do we do next? I know one thing is for certain, Courtney is setting up another tea party and I am invited.

CHAPTER II

Home; Dazed And Confused

(March 27, 2001)

(I have been able to sleep more when I am work than I do at home. Kim has been absolutely unbelievable. When I am at work, she takes care of Courtney and Nathaniel. I have been feeling so bad for Courtney. She is only 2 years old and puts up with so much already. I am starting to feel we do not do enough for her. She keeps herself busy and entertains herself very well. That box in which the TV came in has been awesome, she plays in it all of the time. Kim and myself are struggling though, I see it in Kim's eyes when I come home. She is tired and frustrated.)

I. Home: A place where one lives; a place where memories are made; where one can find physical and emotional warmth; to call his or her own.

II. Nathaniel's Home: A trying expedition of keeping one's wits about themselves all the while raising Courtney. Crying, I mean a lot of crying. Not just by Nathaniel, mommy and daddy are crying, too.

Where the hell do I begin now? Looking back on it all now (6 years later) how did we survive as a family. Nathaniel's crying was so upsetting. No matter what we did, nothing worked. The crying would get to us so easily. Our pediatrician told us if things get too rough to bear, lay Nathaniel down in his bassinet and you have to walk away. So Kim and I made this a rule that must be followed. We cannot let ourselves be pushed over the edge. On the flip side, another tough part was when Nathaniel was not crying. He was emotionless. No smiles, no crying just a troubling stare with his eyes flickering back and forth. Courtney would try her hardest to play with Nathaniel and get him to smile, but to no avail. His look was painful, or like he was confused. Every picture we took of him, he had the same painful expression if he was not crying. The craziest thing of all, and to this day we cannot explain it, when we were taking pictures of him they all turned out blurry. Only Nathaniel. If Kim, Courtney or myself were in the picture we were clear, but Nathaniel had a haze around him. I thought it was the film we were using but we changed film and cameras and the same thing happened. Some freaky shit. Kim and I were convinced there were angels around him, we hope. As each day past in Drexel Hill, PA we became more unsettled. No matter how we held or carried Nathaniel, he would cry. An ear-piercing wail at times. There was no consoling him. Our days and nights became one. Kim and I would take turns putting Courtney to bed at night. Courtney was given a trundle bed handed down from her great Aunt Lorrie and Uncle Rick. The bottom would pull out with a mattress on it for a second bed. Kim and I would enjoy these treasured moments. Not just for having bedtime with Courtney, but we would get as much sleep as possible. All the while, one of us would be with Nathaniel in the master bedroom. We would always start off with a bottle. Five or six ounces would take forever to finish because he would forget how to drink, this would frustrate Nathaniel, and the crying would begin. By the way, Kim and I would like to thank the inventor of the pacifier. Nathaniel would always need something to suck on to get him settled. It may have not been for long, but it helped.

As he rested and starts to fall asleep, the sucking on his pacifier would slow down and we would think, "He is falling asleep, maybe a deep sleep. This could be the night." But as soon as we laid him down, he would startle and start crying again. If we did get him settled in his bassinet, as soon as we turned out the light or the TV, he was back awake crying. This ritual started from the very first night home. We would start this every night at 9:00 or 10:00 PM until the next morning. We would split the shift the majority of the time. Some nights Kim or I would go until morning to help the other try to get a full night's sleep. Sometimes, I would let Nathaniel sleep on my chest in bed with me. Of course, this is something, as a parent we were not supposed to do, but it was the only way to survive at times. It may only work for an hour and a half, but

Nathaniel would need it. Daddy would need it because we knew there was no other way for sleep.

As these long and agonizing nights came to their end things would get worse because it was time for me to go to work. The feelings I had leaving Kim home alone with the kids would make me sick, even guilty. If she was up at all during the night before, I do not know how she did it. I ran a floor covering store for a local family. My schedule was Tuesday's and Thursday's I would work from 9:30 AM to 8:00 PM, Wednesday's and Friday's I would work from 9:30 AM to 5:30 PM and Saturday's from 10:00 AM to 5:00 PM. I had Sunday's and Monday's off together. Some days were longer if I had to measure houses before or after work. I did work the majority of the time by myself. We did not have a ton of customers, but we wrote a sale on every customer that came through the door. I wrote my sales, did my paperwork and took naps as often as possible.

By the time I got home, I usually found Kim in the recliner, exhausted. But she tried to make everything as normal as possible. Dinner was on, the living room and dining room, where Courtney played all day long was usually clean. I would tell her; "leave it and I will take care of it." Sometimes, I would feel very inadequate for Kim. My feeling was that I had to step up more. I still love playing hockey, but I now realize that I will have to give it up and give more rest time to Kim.

After seeing Nathaniel's doctor at DuPont Children's Hospital, we still do not know what to think. This neurologist was a cold person. He said everything to us in medical lingo and seemed to be frustrated with us when we did not understand him. We had visited this hospital before after Courtney's birth. Courtney was so long when she was born, she was cramped up in mommy's belly that she had a dislocated hip. So when we were taking Courtney home for the first time, we were told to go directly to DuPont so she can be fitted for a harness to keep her legs in a certain position to let her hip heal. When we were at Courtney's appointment, I said to Kim, "Be thankful we do not have to come here on a regular basis." Not realizing, this was our first glimpse into the fraternity of families with disabilities.

We tried to put the pieces together ourselves a lot of the time. We were told unofficially that Nathaniel could be diagnosed down the road with Cerebral Palsy, which is defined as simply as a condition caused by brain damage around the time of birth that may be marked by the lack of muscle control, especially in the limbs. I guess there can be no official diagnoses until Nathaniel gets a little older. On top of everything, Nathaniel sounds like he has a touch of colic. This, of course would make him cry more. His seizures are still present but not as bad since he is taking his medication, but it is so damn hard to give it to him. It has this strong peppermint flavor. He chokes on it all of the time. We were told to mix it with one ounce of his formula. Still he has trouble swallowing because of the colic. Years later we figured out all of the crying also had to do with him starving to death. Nathaniel was not getting enough of his formula. It was just one thing after another. Then we started to notice Nathaniel's eyes, constantly shuffling back and forth all of the time. This is very upsetting because when we look at him we can tell he cannot see us properly. He will not follow your finger or a light in front of his eyes. Blindness. What next? Yes, there are times he is, to a certain extent, OK. He does sit quietly in our arms in the rocker recliner and he even gets very relaxed, too. Still at a drop of a hat, he can go ballistic. This is what makes everything so nerve racking. When will things change? At any moment, he can blow up again.

(April 1, 2001)

(I do not know what to do any more. No direct answers from anyone. I feel we are alone in this situation. I feel like they want to say, "he is a brain-damaged child, what do you want us to do? Give us a straight answer. What can we expect? What are we doing right? What are we doing wrong?" No one says anything. Like they are protecting each other's ass. I do not know how we are doing what we are doing. Kim and I do not sleep any more. The neighbors must think we are bad parents. I know they hear the crying. The other day Kim needed to walk away and breathe, Nathaniel's crying would not stop, so she went outside with Courtney for some fresh air. She went a few houses down to the neighbors, who were outside, and she said all that you heard was Nathaniel crying throughout the neighborhood.)

Reliving as I write. Of course there are certain things I never want to relive but in this case, I must. I want people to hear me. I want people to hear Nathaniel. There is a young boy trapped in a damaged body. As

I relive the crying I want people to hear the screams come up off these pages. I want my words to pierce everyone's ears. No one person should be labeled. No one should have to live this way. But we do, every day. We did not ask for all of this. Kim had very normal pregnancies with Courtney and Nathaniel. Every prenatal visit was as normal as can be. She does everything that is asked of her. So we held up our end of the bargain. But other people did not. So now, we are starting on this journey that, at times, some doctors and nurses that we visit, look at us as if we exaggerate when we tell them what is going on at home. One nurse actually said to me one time "Come on now, it cannot be that bad." I just sat there and looked at her as if she was exaggerating when she said it. You know, give her a taste of her own medicine. But no, she kept right on writing Nathaniel's chart up for the doctor. She knew I was staring right through her but she would not look up at me, nor did she say anything else. I believe that until you walk in one's shoes, keep your mouth shut.

On the opposite end of the spectrum, we had a very cute elderly couple living next to us, James and Doris. Doris was sick a lot, so James did everything for her, always running to pick up prescriptions or running Doris to her doctor appointments. We talked often. I use to apologize for Nathaniel's crying. James would say to me, "Chris, we don't hear a thing as far as you know, but we can tell by yours and Kimberly's faces that you are troubled and tired." James always threw in a dig at me once and a while, but always knew what to say. I always told him, "You got that right!" They always checked on us to see if we needed anything or if we needed them to go to the store for us or how about some prayers? I would tell them prayers were the best medicine.

And we need every prayer possible. I joked a couple of times about maybe even an exorcism. I just wish Nathaniel could snap out of this whole mess. I knew times were going to be tough, but this is turning out to be ridiculous. I started to feel we really needed a break. But, who do we trust with Nathaniel? I mean if we ask someone to watch the kids and Nathaniel is going crazy, whoever is watching him may not know what to do or they may never want to help watch them again. Or, if it is a family member, we would be disowned.

Kim's cousin's wedding was coming up and we thought this would be a great opportunity to get out together for the first time since "Thaniel" was born. Still I do not know who I should ask. A week before the wedding, my brother Jimmy called and said that he and my sister-in-law Terry thought maybe Kim and I needed a break and offered to watch the kids. Timing could not have been better, so I took them up on their offer. Nervously, I did. It was great to get a chance to get out, and then my mind started to race. What if this?, What if that?, then I started to think, "we cannot go out, forget about it!" I called them back and told them "Thanks, but no thanks." But to them the answer was "Go!" "Yes you are going out, no questions asked." I asked them if they were sure about 100 times.

So we are going out. Together. Husband and wife. Nervously. Did I say that already? See, I told you we are nervous. When they arrived, we were ready to paint the town. We told them over and over where everything was and what to do if something happens and my cell phone number is . . . They just looked at us and said, "Go!" Yeah, but . . . "Go!" "Just Go!" So go we did. We were so excited to see everyone. (The majority of Kim's family lives in Maryland, but her cousin was marrying a girl from our neck of the woods so the reception was only 15 minutes from our house.) It was wonderful to be out with adults. Everyone said we looked great. But a few could tell we were emotionally spent. I could not remember how many times I told people about what had happened to Nathaniel and what we are going through now. I tried not to dwell on it. All I wanted to do was for Kim to forget about everything, enjoy the moment, and enjoy the company of her family, for we do not know what will be going on next.

When we arrived back at home, we joked before we got out of the van about hearing Nathaniel screaming throughout the neighborhood. So we get out of the car, not a sound. Not a sound walking up to the house. Not a sound as we opened the front door. Courtney ran up to us and said, "Quiet, Thaniel is sleeping!" What is going on here? "No way," I thought. Jimmy and Terry were sitting on the couch while Nathaniel was sleeping in his portable bassinet. On his side. "On his side?" We never laid him on his side before. They were geniuses. Give them the Nobel Peace Prize because there is peace in our house for the first time since Nathaniel came home. This has to be something new to try. I must tell you it worked. It was not the be all to end all, but the percentages went up from about 4 percent to 12 percent for him to stay asleep when we lay him down. Any new thing helps. The next thing I think we have to work on was to keep that pacifier in his mouth. This is his sleep mechanism. This night out also brought us a chance for a new start and maybe some much needed help.

(April 8, 2001)

(It is the day after Kim's cousin's wedding. We had a wonderful time and enjoyed the time out. Something else happened that is very interesting to me. Kim's uncle wanted to talk to me. After the reception, the whole family was going back to the hotel they were staying at, they were going to hang out at the bar for a few drinks and cigars and Kim's uncle wanted to talk business. So I met up with him. He is offering a position in his business in Gaithersburg, MD. This means we would have to move. From what I understand is that the state of Maryland would be better for Nathaniel. Through my healthcare plan at work and through the state. This is really something to ponder.)

Listen, I never moved more than 10 miles from where I grew up in Broomall, PA. This was going to be a huge change in our lives if we accept. I was invited to come down and check out their business and would give me the low down on how everything works. Kim knows the area pretty well. She is from Maryland and maybe she will feel more comfortable as she will be closer to family members. In our circumstance, family and friends can only do so much. It's not that I do not trust them; it's that I do not want to burden them with taking care of a sick child. And I am not talking about a cough and cold sick child. I mean a brain-damaged-with-seizures sick child. It is hard enough for us to deal with Nathaniel; I cannot and will not put that pressure on someone else.

So can we do this move? This was a hard decision to make. Kim wants to make sure I am OK before we decide, but the question is when? When can we do this? My work situation is already taken care of, so no job hunting. We need to find a place to live. I think this is the biggest hurdle. One of us will have to go down and house hunt and we would have to rent because of previous credit problems. You know the same old story. Young, stupid and with credit cards. I believe we can find someone nice to help us out so we can get on track. It is about to turn June and we also have to think about setting aside money for the move and probably for the first and last month's rent. All the while paying rent where we live now. So how long will this take? And for now, we have to focus on Nathaniel because his baptism is fast approaching.

(June 3, 2001)

(Nathaniel was baptized yesterday. Kim's uncle Rick and my sister Kathy are his godparents. This was our first adventure out as a family with Nathaniel. There were seven babies being baptized this day. We were third in line. Nathaniel was actually asleep when we arrived. But when he woke up, the crying returned. At first, it was OK, but soon Nathaniel proceeded to cry at a full blown roar the rest of the time we were there. After he was baptized, we tried to stay, but Nathaniel was out of control. We were so embarrassed. The other families were looking at us. I felt we were ruining this special day for everyone. Father Curran, who baptized Nathaniel, called us to see if everything was OK. He did not know Nathaniel was sick, and asked if he could come and visit us for some prayers.)

I am the guy who yelled at God a couple of months ago and here I stand for the first time in his church since the birth of Nathaniel. What's wrong with me? I am so back and forth, about how I feel about why God allowed what happened to Nathaniel. I do not know how to feel yet. My emotions are going crazy. I feel at times I should not be in a church for what I said and other times I know God is allowing me forgiveness and letting me find my way back in. This baptism is a train wreck to me. Nathaniel will not stop crying, and six other families with children being baptized are staring at us like "can you please shut that kid up?" I was mortified. I just could not wait to leave. I felt we ruined this day for other families. My sister Kathy and uncle Rick were doing their best to control Nathaniel. My head was spinning. I kept praying for him to stop, but he kept getting louder and louder. All of this going on made me feel more distant from God. I just wanted to get out of there and never see these people again. I also started to think that we can never go out as a family again. We will be looked upon everywhere we go and we would ruin someone else's day. We are going to do this separately from now on. One of us will stay home with Nathaniel.

The unfortunate thing was that we never got a chance to meet up with Father Curran. He was feeling there was something wrong and there was a reason behind the crying. I explained to him what happened to

Nathaniel at birth and he now understood. He also felt my resistance and my anguish. He wanted so much to visit just to say hi or maybe offer some prayers were in order. We never had a chance to get together, but five years later one of my cousin's was getting married in the same church and out walked Father Curran. I felt I had to talk to him. So after the wedding I introduced myself and asked him if he remembered us. He did. "I recall a young man who cried extremely hard and loud." He said. "You cannot forget a cry like that one." He said a prayer for us and hoped we were getting better.

(June 23, 2001)

(My mom, Aunt Pat and my sister Kathy want us to move in with them so we can save money for a move to Maryland. It will be a tight fit but this is the only way we can move.)

I guess God is answering some of my questions. I still do not know what to think. Moving in with mom, Pat and Kathy will be interesting. But we must save for a move. The helping hands do work. My sister let Kim and I go out a couple of times together. These nights out felt like first dates. Courtney and "Kacky" hit it off, of course. They are like sisters. Courtney had a chance to do things with "Kacky" that mom and dad did not have a chance to catch until it was too late. Aunt Pat is the other big sister. Mom mom would try to lay down the rules and would limit Courtney in things she can do and touch. "Kacky" and Pat would bend those rules as far as they could go.

I finally had to give up on my work. The hours were hard to handle and my work was suffering. I worked for Fisher's Carpet One in Edgemont, PA. The Fisher's were a wonderful family to work with. It is rare in today's world to work for a family-owned business and feel you are a part of that family. For that, I am forever grateful. Kim is an disabled Army girl and was receiving benefits, so we were not drowning yet. But I thought after being home all of the time, a part-time job will help, and it did. We lived on the living room floor, making beds out of the couch and chair cushions. Just like before, Kim and I would take turns with Nathaniel every night. For the first time family members would see what we go through in a 24 hour period. As I start to think about our move, I realize we will be on our own again. From what I understand, with the benefits from work and the state of Maryland, things should be better. I do not know how, but we will see. We were told that the doctors would be better to deal with than PA. Come to think of it, anything would be better than PA. That bad taste in my mouth, I wish it on no one. The State of PA did nothing to help Nathaniel or us. It was beyond my comprehension how difficult everything became. It was like pulling teeth to get answers.

In late July, Kim's aunt called and said she found a house in Frederick, MD for rent. We need to move on it quickly because it was in a community everyone wanted to get into. So Kim left by herself that night to stay with her aunt and uncle so she can look at the house the very next day as early in the morning as possible. Well, she loved it and it was a price we could handle. And it is available in September. So our minds are made up and we are packing up our stuff. Our lives are about to change drastically. As September approached and the reality of moving to central Maryland came closer, I reflected back on my life on where I grew up and how I grew up. I was only moving two and a half hours away, but Frederick, MD was at a total different pace. And as you will read later, I have grown to love that pace. Going back, I played it safe. Stayed out of trouble, for the most part. Played a ton of hockey with my nephews Eric and Gary (my sister Kathy's oldest two kids), scalped tickets to a ton of Flyers games with them. Also played a lot of hockey with the Blue Devils (you guys know who you are) I loved the way you guys fulfilled my hockey dreams. I did not smoke (tried it one time, it sucked) and no drugs at all. Every part of my life up until February 14, 2001, was a joy to experience and would live it all over again if I had the chance. But from that day forward until Sept. 5, 2001, it was a complete blur in PA. We were not taught anything about how to take care of a brain damaged child. The excruciating painful knot in my stomach will be there to the day I die. I will always have a tear in my eye for "Thaniel" especially when I think of who he could have become. My dreams for him are gone. The only way I will get to know who he is will be when I meet him in heaven, that is if I get there after what I have said and thought to God and my mom. I would love to invite all of you who dropped Nathaniel's life through your hands, to Kim and I have grown during this unfortunate experience to love each other more and cherish our children even closer. I hope I can reach out and touch one life with what I write so they can feel what Kim and I feel. Unfortunately it took a tragic accident at birth to bring us even closer. We were on the way to being that close already. We have made it so far. Sometimes I do not know how. Maybe a change of scenery will bring hope. Maybe a blessing in disguise. I am scared but willing. I love my family. We have to make this work. Now!

CHAPTER III

Hectic New Beginnings

If you think our lives have been crazy since Nathaniel has been born, you have not read anything yet. Our turbulent times were all about the injury to Nathaniel for the past six months. Everything else has been pretty smooth. Well forget about that now. So buckle up, this is going to be a bumpy ride.

It all starts out with our townhouse not being ready because the previous renters messed it up pretty good so it needed to be painted and the carpet to be cleaned. So I had no choice but to put or stuff into storage for now in Maryland. Then I moved in with Kim's aunt Dorney. Kim and the kids are staying in PA at my mom's house until our house is ready. I have to start working. On my forth day at work, Sept. 11, 2001, well we all know what happened that day. My office is 27 miles from the Pentagon working next to the Gaithersburg Air Field watching U.S. troops and the county police close down the airfield as F-16 fighters fly overhead. Back in PA, Kim had a long night with Nathaniel so she sleeps through all of the events until noon. I tried calling her but the lines were busy until late afternoon. It was refreshing to hear her voice. So to feel more comfortable the next weekend Kim and the kids moved down to stay with her aunt also.

We finally moved in on Sept. 22 to our new home. It feels great to get settled. But suddenly the following week Kim is admitted to the hospital. She has Crohn's Disease and is having problems with her belly. Here I am already calling out of work; it's a different state but the same old story. The doctor says she will be in the hospital for a couple of days. While she is in, I start to meet some of the neighbors. I noticed there are many kids around, so Courtney is fitting right in. The second day Kim was in the hospital I was pushing Courtney on the swing in the playground out behind our house, all the while Nathaniel is resting on my shoulder. A woman approaches me and says, "Why don't you leave your kids here and go visit your wife in the hospital?" The first words out of my mouth were "And you are?" This is my first encounter with Brenda De La Cruz. Brenda is one of a kind. I have to admit to this day she is one of the truest friends Kim and I have met since moving to Maryland. But at this very first moment I met her I thought, "Who the hell is this woman and get her away from my children." No really, I did think it. Kim had met her and another neighbor, Shaun, and talked often with them. Today I love Brenda dearly. She is my BGFF (Best Girl Friend Forever). She has been with us through the ups and downs. And she helps us when we need back up, and of course, that goes vice versa with her kids, too.

So Kim comes home and is feeling better after some rest and a new medication. A couple of weeks later, on Monday, Oct. 22 I am in a car accident at work. I have a broken right leg, slightly broken left elbow and a totaled car. I must have surgery to fix my leg. They have to put a rod from my ankle to my knee and will be in the hospital for the rest of the week. I come home with a specially designed walker to get around with because my arm is in a cast up to my shoulder and I cannot use crutches yet. Since we live in a townhouse, I have a hospital bed in between the living room and dining room because surely I cannot go up and down the stairs. I feel like the biggest burden to Kim. When I get home from the hospital, she looks so tired, but she just goes on because we have too.

The following Monday, Nathaniel gets very sick and is having seizures. He is taken to Children's Hospital in Washington, D.C. Courtney goes to Kim's sister Kelly's house. For the next week, I am home alone. Broken leg, broken elbow, funky walker. Thank God for my physical therapist and Brenda. The therapist would get me up and exercising and help me set up for the rest of the afternoon, and Brenda would pick up her kids at Shaun's and come over make dinner and get me set up for the night. My days went like this: From hospital bed to bathroom to recliner to bathroom to hospital bed. Thank God, the World Series was on that week or I would have gone crazy. At the same time at Children's Hospital, doctors are trying to regulate Nathaniel's seizures before he comes home, and Courtney is having a great time at Aunt Kelly's. I guess when it gets drastic like it has since we moved; we can bend but not break. Except for me. We keep moving forward. Very, very slowly, but forward.

(November 3, 2001)

(Kim called from Children's Hospital and said the doctor has some ideas on what tests to perform on Nathaniel. I said, "Who does?" She said, "His neurologist." He has a neurologist? Children's Hospital is on the ball. He has a team of doctors checking on him. This is more than anything we saw in PA. We are going to set up appointments with each doctor in their specific fields of care so we can learn what is really going on inside Nathaniel.)

Doctors here in Maryland and in Washington, D.C. seem genuine and more interested in taking care of Nathaniel. They show their concern, and that makes us feel better. When we are all back home, things go back to normal. I mean "our normal". At least my cast is off my arm and I can handle Nathaniel. I asked Kim to put Nathaniel's portable crib next to the recliner so I can take care of him at night. Listen, Kim and I sleep with one eye shut and one ear open, but still Kim jumps out of bed when she barely hears him or when he is ballistic. I try to tell her to get lost, but she still comes down anyway. I was not going to win these battles. I am in no condition to force her back up to bed. But when I do get him calm, I can lean over the recliner and put him in his crib then I can hobble over to the hospital bed and go to bed. I can jump up to settle him if he stirs or I can get up in the recliner and rock him back to sleep.

The one thing that helps us before the holidays was that the accident I was in was someone else's fault. So the insurance company paid off our totaled car. And the girl who caused the accident, her insurance company paid out for the damages and medical bills. But the type of insurance I have for Nathaniel already paid my bills. So we had a very good Christmas. After the New Year, I bought a new car and went back to work still hobbling. Then we started to get information through the state of Maryland. Nathaniel was enrolled into the Infants and Toddlers program (same as PA, but down here in MD they actually show up) in which people come to the house and provide different therapies for Nathaniel. He also has been designated a caseworker from the state and through her we were finding different options and helpful organizations to help Nathaniel. This is when we found out we were entitled to in-home nursing help. No way! Get the hell out of here! Really? We can have nurses help us? Here they can come out and check up on him, which I thought was great so we can see how we are doing or they can teach us how to do specific things when they make their visits. Kim says, "No Chris, not visits. Shift work." I said, "You mean a nurse will come out and does an eight-hour shift of our choosing? No way? Get the hell out of here? Really? We can have nurses help us like that? YES! It is about freakin' time! Where have you been, Maryland, all of Nathaniel's life?

Now we have to figure out when we want the nurses to come out. Kim says, "That is a no brainer of course. Overnight." I said, "You mean we can go to bed while a nurse takes care of Nathaniel? I wonder what that feels like. Kim and I have not slept together by ourselves in the same room since Feb. 13, 2001. Oh yes, I have been counting. This could be very invigorating to get a strong seven to eight hours of sleep especially next to my beautiful wife. Just thinking of it makes me very excited. We can start to function better, I know it. So we get to meet the head of the nursing agency and fill out a ton of paperwork. And I mean a ton. Every question had to be answered twice about what has been going on since birth, and it was hard on Kim. She really hates reliving Nathaniel's short past. We requested a night nurse from midnight to 8 in the morning. Of course, the agency had to search for a while to find a nurse to fill the full time shift and a nurse for part time. It took a couple of weeks but we have found a nurse for full time to start. He came out to orientate and seemed very nice. On his first night out, we were as nervous as first time parents. This will be the first time one of us is not staying with Nathaniel overnight since he came home from the hospital. But it was hard to walk away. The nurse said don't worry, he can handle it. So we went to bed, still I slept with one eye shut and one ear open. We kept opening the door to take a listen. We had to learn to go to sleep all over again. We did notice something, when we finally were settled, the nurse was on his cell phone, which I did not think was appropriate for him to do. The next morning, Nathaniel was crying, what's new, so I started to get ready for work, when I was ready to come down I heard the nurse on his cell phone again, but he was hurrying off the call to pick up Nathaniel. Kim and I noticed this pattern for the first two nights, so Kim let the agency know and they would talk to him about it.

Well the third night things got down right bizarre. He came 20 minutes late into the house on his cell phone and he was not very happy. I had to wait about five minutes for him to get off the phone call so I could tell him what kind of day Nathaniel had. Finally, when he was done he apologized and we talked.

After our conversation, he seemed to be more on the ball this night. I went to bed. What happened next blew our minds. As soon as he thought we were asleep, he was back on the phone with someone and very upset with them. Kim and I caught the conversation and determined he was fighting with his girlfriend or wife about him seeing his ex-wife all of the time. This episode went on for an hour and a half. He had to go. We asked the agency to remove him. I mean he was not giving Nathaniel any attention and he would be hurrying to pick up Nathaniel when he heard us coming downstairs. I started to think we couldn't catch a break even with nurses. This is a chance for help, but we need a stronger effort. We finally got it with our next set of nurses and the nights have become peaceful and restful for the Breen family.

(April 3, 2002)

(Kim and Nathaniel left today for North Carolina. I hope she can do this trip and the three-week stay without my help. Mom and Aunt Pat have come to help out with Courtney when I go to work. But I cannot stop thinking of Kim.)

Not to say we are desperate or looking for a miracle, but we have been searching for different options on the World Wide Web. We thought maybe we could find organizations or some type of vitamins or medicine we can try. Kim came across an article on kids and adults who are getting treatments in a hyperbaric chamber to help with stroke victims and brain injuries. We searched for tests and studies done on people and the results were encouraging. For us, it so happens the closest chamber open to the public was in North Carolina and of course, it was not covered under any medical insurance organizations and the FDA (Food and Drug Administration) has not given their thumbs up on this type of treatment. There were a couple of different plans we can choose from. The most reasonable was a 21 day stay with two treatments daily. The cost, $5,500.00. So I wrote a letter to family and friends for their support and asked to open their charitable hearts. They did. Kim drove the nine hours to North Carolina with Nathaniel. How? I don't know. Now, the treatment process is cool. Nathaniel and Kim would go in this chamber, which sat about eight people so they would share their time with others with disabilities. With the door shut and sealed, the pressure would drop to simulate being under 30 feet of water. (The U.S. Military, especially the Navy would use the chamber for divers who had decompression sickness and it would help them adjust back to sea level.) When the pressure reached the target depth, a halo ring was put around Nathaniel's head and an astronaut like clear helmet would be attached. After the connection, pure oxygen is pumped into Nathaniel's helmet for the next hour. Nathaniel would breathe in the fresh air. A lot of these studies we searched showed, with this action taken it could help the person with the disability and their neurological symptoms rejuvenate damaged brain cells or help kick-start brain cell not even being used. The medical community and its "politics" have researchers going into these studies with very negative attitudes about hyperbaric oxygen. I guess the studies are up in the air right now (no pun intended). Now remember, I said we were not looking for a miracle but something like this could help, and it did. After 22 exhausting days away, Kim and Nathaniel came home and we see something that has changed. Nathaniel has Cortical Blindness, which is the total loss or partial loss of vision in a normal-appearing eye caused by damage to the visual area in the brain's optical cortex. In blue-collar terms, Nathaniel has partial vision, like he is looking through a slice of Swiss cheese or he may only see shadows. After being home, we noticed Nathaniel was focusing better and he would follow us as we walked in front of him. He was a little slow tracking us but he was tracking. And he has been smiling these days. You can tell he is more relaxed and not so mixed up. The crying is less and hopefully leaving.

(April 29, 2002)

(Nathaniel is scheduled for three tests at Children's Hospital today. Maybe there are more defining answers after these tests. I am always scared to hear answers about Nathaniel, but if I think about it, we never really got answers especially when we lived in PA. I am so glad to meet these doctors; they really seem to care and want to find answers for us. Let us hope.)

My knowledge of medical terminology has increased since Nathaniel's birth and I can have some meaningful conversations with doctors and understand what they say. Hay, I still ask for those simplified answers once and a while, but for the first time some words are new to our ears. Since Nathaniel was already in the hospital with seizure activity and the off and on ear piercing crying, his doctors want Nathaniel to have a 24 hour E.E.G., otherwise known as an Electroencephalogram. But there is one stipulation for the parents, they are asking us not to stay in the hospital with him. Go home and get some rest. The one thing they want to do is observe Nathaniel without Kim or myself coddling him. The thought is to get the full range of Nathaniel's seizures and crying episodes without mom and dad there to pick him up. To help ease our minds, he is put in a room next to the nurses' station so they could be right there for him.

By this time, Nathaniel was having a following of nurses that would check on him even if he was not on their rotation of patients when working or they would stop by when their shift ended. They all say it is his eyelashes. They are jealous of his long eyelashes. I must say he has a beautiful set of lashes that he uses to his advantage. He hooks in those female nurses. I feel I have trained him well. Or as Kim would say, maybe he could teach me a lesson or two.

When Kim and I return two days later, we again were surprised. He was asleep, on his back with no pacifier. I jokingly asked where was my son or how much sleeping medication did they give him? We talked to the neurologist about his E.E.G. and we really did not like what came next. Nathaniel has so much brain damage, he only has about one quarter of the brain we have. The rest of his brain was basically dormant of brain activity. The quarter of brain that is functional shows a lot of mixed up signals. We have kind of figured this out already but to hear those words, it hurt. It took me back to the night Kim went to the hospital and we felt something was wrong. I started to question myself again why didn't I speak up or throw a fit in the hospital that night and we would not be in this mess.

The doctors also did blood work to check his medication levels and they were off a little so that can account for his seizure count rising. So there is something we can adjust. Nathaniel also saw a gastroenterologist doctor while he was in and she was looking at his formula intake and weight gain. They did a swallow test and Nathaniel fails miserable. So more visits are set up for the occupational therapist to help with his motor skills, especially using his mouth.

So not all news was bad, but the bad news blew away the good news. So what now? After hearing the devastating results of the E.E.G. what can we look forward to in the future? Kim put it best, "We love him!" "We do the same thing we have been doing and we love him even more." I do not know if Kim remembers saying these words, but I never forgotten them. This is all we can do. There may be things out there that will help, but his brain injury will never go away. Hearing Kim's words finally made me realize this is it. This is our lives as long as Nathaniel is alive. At first it hurt. But I started to think about who hurts more: us or Nathaniel? We have to resign ourselves to this fact and step up. As you read this paragraph I look at the clock on the cable box and it is 12:53 AM on Tuesday, July 31, 2007. I wrote the specific time and date for you to understand one thing. I STEPPED UP! Somewhere along the way I realized this is not about me feeling bad or sorry for myself and Kimberly as parents. We are a family. So there is something different about what we do or how we go about doing these things. So what, we are starting to figure this out. We can do this thing they call life. Hearing the neurologist's words hurt, but we have to go on.

Nathaniel stayed in the hospital a couple more days and when I went to visit him after work one day; I was told I could take him home. I said, "Great!" I was lucky enough to have stopped at home and I decided to drive our van to the hospital so I had his car seat with me so we can go home. I called Kim and gave her the good news. So Nathaniel and I packed up and started home. The ride home is normally a little over an hour. But this night, wow. Nathaniel did not like riding in a car, van, whatever. At one point in time we took out the middle bench of our van so we could put his portable bassinet on the floor so he could sleep lying down on long trips. So I get about 10 minutes down the road and Nathaniel is starting to fuss. I reach back and grab his hand to let him know I am here and everything is OK. Also you have to remember at the hospital the nurses and doctors have Nathaniel off his pacifiers so we are driving by the seat of our pants for the trip home. Off and on he is crying. I am driving one handed, one on the wheel and one hand holding Nathaniel's hand in the back seat. I get past the D.C. beltway and start heading up route 270 north towards Frederick. About a 35 minute trip with no traffic, four days with traffic. It was about 7:30 PM on a Friday night. The weekend escape traffic has settled down and we are moving on up the road but Nathaniel is crying more now. So I pull off in Rockville, MD, get him out of his seat and calm him down and change a diaper. As soon as I get Nathaniel back in his seat the fussing starts immediately. I get a couple miles up the road and pull off in Gaithersburg, MD to calm him down again. I call Kim on the phone and she could hear Nathaniel better than she can hear me. I told her we were stopping again so he can settle and so Kim would not be worrying where we were.

After a short break I am back on the road and I have to pull off the road in Germantown, MD, and the same thing is going on. I am just trying to relax Nathaniel as best I can. The stress is tremendous. Again, I am heading up the road but this time I have to get Nathaniel out of the car all together. I pull off in Urbana, MD. Nathaniel is ballistic, almost to the point of hyperventilating. I am a little stir crazy by this point, but I am not mad or frustrated. Well maybe a little frustrated. In my new found way of looking at things, my focus was totally on Nathaniel. Not what am "I" going to do? It is what can "I" do for you, Nathaniel? I held him tight to my chest and I felt his heart racing and he was sweating like crazy. I walked around the van for about 15 minutes or so to calm him down. The connection I felt with him this night was invigorating. I got him to calm down. I kept telling him, "Daddy is here and nothing is going to hurt you. I am here for you." I could have had someone walk up and pull a gun and try to rob us and I would not have noticed it. And if someone did try this I would have gotten the gun away from him and beaten that person senseless with it for ruining our moment. I asked Nathaniel to calm down in the most calming voice I had. There was this calm over the two of us. I did it! He still was giving a bit of a whimper and he was trying to catch his breath like a small child does after a long, hard cry. His head was on my shoulder as I peeked around to see what he was doing; he was just looking around taking it all in. Quietly. Like "my dad is holding me and I feel comfortable right where I am." I also knew as soon as I put him in his car seat, things will change drastically. So I made a decision that was so illegal, it would make Britney Spears look like a saint for driving around with her kids not buckled in. I realized it was almost completely dark out so I called Kim and told her where I was and what I plan to do. She told me to do it. Get home any way I can. So I figured out where I was I would only have to travel on a main road for about three to four miles and the rest of the way home can be on back roads. Nathaniel and I decided he would feel better right where he was in my arms with his head on my shoulder. So I strapped the two of us into the driver seat and waited to pull out of the park and ride when there were no cars in site and hope there were no police around also. So out we go, down the road towards the only light I need to go through until I reach our community. Hoping the light would stay green so we do not have to stop and have someone pull up beside us and see what I am doing. It stays green. We keep moving all the way to the front door of our townhouse. Not a peep out of Nathaniel all the way home. Like he knew he could trust his dad to get him there. I told him, "Do not get use to this boy." Kim met us at the car and took Nathaniel inside as I continued to sit there. I began to cry. I was exhausted emotionally and physically. But I felt strong, even empowered. The accomplishment of what we did, no matter how illegal it may have been, I connected with my son. How beautiful is that. It was 9:50 p.m., two hours and twenty minutes after leaving Children's Hospital. The longest two twenty of my life.

(June 19, 2002)

(Nathaniel was really having a hard time swallowing and the doctors decided to put a G-Tube down his nose into his belly. It was taped to his cheek and nose. Maybe since he has this hard time getting his formula and medicine, the tube will help bypass right to his belly. I hope his seizures will go away.)

Do you ever think about how many times a day you swallow? Most of the time it is done without thought. It is a mechanism we take for granted. We need it for our nature to survive. Well Nathaniel cannot do this for his for survival. Now he has what they call a G-Tube (Gastric Tube) down his nose and into his belly. The tube gets hooked up to a feeding pump. Nathaniel has to have this tube, he is not getting enough nutrition and his medication is hard to swallow by mouth. Now we have to be careful not to yank this damn thing out of his tummy when we move him around and we have to check the placement of the tube in his belly. It is not hard to put it back it just freaks me out. Nathaniel's pediatrician is worried about his weight and growth. The thing I notice the most is the size of his head, very small in circumference. It looks like Nathaniel is not growing into his body properly. Hopefully he can get what he needs with the placement of the G-Tube. Seeing Nathaniel next to a boy his same age he looks only

2/3 the size of a normal child. Very frail. His legs and arms are skinny with high muscle tone with his arms pulled tight to his chest. His legs have tremors. Nathaniel is now being put on medication to help bring down the high muscle tone. Since the start of the medication he did become less rigid, which I think and I hope will help with the crying. When he was very rigid, the only way I could explain it would be like having a full body "Charlie horse.". If I or you had a full body Charlie horse we would be crying, too. Some of these questions we have are being answered and it does make us feel better about Nathaniel's situation, but it is so hard to think about what could have been. It always comes back to haunt me.

(August 30, 2002)

(Most of the crying is over now. The crying Nathaniel has now is more like a normal child crying, not that full-blown wail. He really seems to be settling down too. The house does not have that ringing sound from the crying. Don't get me wrong, when he gets upset he still wails away, but it is more manageable now because he can be consoled a lot easier. Courtney was worried why Nathaniel was not crying all of the time. That is how close to normal everything is around here. I had to explain to her that this is better for Nathaniel.)

Baclofen, Prevacid and Phenobarbital seem to be the right combination, for now. Nathaniel seems to be more comfortable and he is easier to handle. His stiffness and rigidity are better. So with this being said, we are going to try and go out as a family. Just down the street to the local Italian restaurant. And you know what, it worked. For the first time in a year and a half my family was one, out in public. One whole family, the Breen family. I was so proud of my boy. I was proud of Courtney also, she showed off her brother to anyone who would listen. I enjoyed a meal with my wife who for the first time in a long while had a chance to look across a table and talk to an adult. Kim says this could be debated at times.

Of course, with all of the craziness of our lives, Kim and I think we need more challenges. So we are pregnant. I mean Kim is pregnant. Back when I asked Kim to marry me, and of course she said yes, we talked about our future together and the question came up from Kim "How many?" I said "How many what?" "Kids?" she said. I was thinking of three, and so was she. No matter what the questions were, we thought alike and this is what makes us so compatible and the reason I would never had made this journey so far with anyone else. The reason for a third child: because we want too. We want to see the interaction with another child with Nathaniel. We are missing out on Nathaniel. Courtney does great with Nathaniel, but she keeps to herself or plays with all of the neighborhood children. She is very busy. She has adjusted very well with everything she had to put up with as a 4 year old. I don't know how much she will remember about her first couple of years with Nathaniel, but I do hope she learns from us and shares what she feels about her brother and her own personal feelings. And then she will have to put up with a baby sister also. Also my mom and Aunt Pat are living with us now so everything is changing.

Nathaniel is changing also. He is putting on some weight and is looking healthier. But since we have been going out a couple of times into the humid and hot air, he has been getting really congested and needs breathing treatments to help break it all up. We have been getting him Botox shots for his arms and legs to help alleviate tightness and his tremors. Our game plan is to keep him comfortable and healthy as possible. I guess from now on we should pick and choose when we go out. But the reason for our first night out was to prove to ourselves we can do this as a family. We are only two blocks from our house. I thought we did quite well. Back to Nathaniel's breathing; this has become a concern lately. When it is hot and humid, you can expect Nathaniel to really get what I call "junky", which is a lot of mucus in the chest and lung areas. Since having all of these ailments, his respiratory system is not as strong as yours or mine. Nathaniel has a lot of deficiencies in his damaged body. But his respiratory is what concerns us the most. So from now on, it has to be cool and dry for Nathaniel to go out. When the seasons change I feel we will have to be concerned with colds and flu symptoms. Just think of it this way, with his respiratory the way it is, each junky episode, cold or flu, could lead to pneumonia or even death. Should one have to worry about these things with a son or daughter this early on in life?

(September 25, 2002)

(Everything was going well for a while and then Nathaniel is showing more seizures. Why can't we stay ahead of the game? He looks healthier with meat on his bones, his crying is just about gone, then this happens. All of the time, one step forward, and two steps back. I have things I want to do with Nathaniel. I want to show off Nathaniel, he is my boy. I am so proud of him.)

I finally have something to do with Nathaniel that we both like. We lie on the floor and watch TV together. I don't know how much he can see but either the shadows or images do catch his eyes. So I put cartoons on for him, you know the basics: Barney, Elmo and The Teletubbies, anything geared to a lot of colors or movements on TV is great. I can see a response out of him. But one day he got so excited he set himself into a seizure. A very strong seizure, strong enough to cause him to get sick and choke on his vomit. This is one of the scariest things I have ever witnessed. Then it happened again twenty 20 minutes later. Kim took him to the hospital and the doctors thought maybe since having the G-Tube for a while and the added weight gain, his Phenobarbital levels were off. So we set a doctor's appointment, get the levels checked and adjusted his medication. But Nathaniel is still having strong seizures and vomiting.

For the second time in this book our plight will be seen first-hand by family members or friends. You can tell people about what you are going through on a daily basis, they believe you but they do not see the true effects of Nathaniel, or I have even heard some say it can't be that bad or they really do not see the day to day ways of our world. It was Halloween night and Kim's Aunt Lorrie and Uncle Rick are over (they came over last Halloween to help give out candy or take Courtney out trick or treating because I had my car accident.) So I put on my Winnie the Pooh costume (Yes, I said Winnie the Pooh, what's it to you?) and took out Courtney and our friend Brenda's kids Alex and Allison. While we were out, Nathaniel began having seizures and vomiting. Projectile vomiting. If we catch it early enough we hold him over the toilet to vomit. By the time we came back from trick or treating, Kim told me what has been going on and maybe we should take him to the hospital. Since these seizures have had the best of Nathaniel for the better part of a month with a few trips to the doctor's office and there is no change in seizures and vomiting pattern, Kim thinks we should go right to Children's Hospital in Washington, D.C. If we go to the hospital here in Frederick they will just transfer us to Children's anyway. As Kim and Nathaniel are getting ready, Nathaniel is having another seizure, so I scoop him up and rush into the bathroom and let him vomit over the toilet. Also, Nathaniel has lost all of the weight he put on and is starting to look frail again. For the first time, I saw sadness in someone else's eyes other than Kim or mine, looking back at myself in the mirror. Aunt Lorrie was upset by what she witnessed and I know Uncle Rick had to feel bad also. Finally, someone witnessed an episode of Nathaniel's uncontrollable life. I do not know what to feel. I just wanted to say, "See!" I tell everyone what happens 24/7 but I feel they truly do not believe us or again they think it cannot be that bad. Yeah, it is that bad. Not to say Lorrie and Rick did not believe us, I just wanted someone to see it first-hand. I guess you can call this my testimony was justified in front of someone other than my wife or myself.

After my feelings of justification have past, we now must focus on what the hell is going on with Nathaniel now. We have been going back and forth to the doctor's offices and the emergency rooms. Things are not changing for the better, they are getting worse. For the last year and a half we have gotten use to Nathaniel's seizures but now they are stronger and it is causing him to vomit and get dehydrated. The pounds keep coming off and Nathaniel is not just worrying mom and dad, the doctors are running out of options. Nathaniel was readmitted to Children's Hospital in DC on Nov. 17th for reoccurring tonic seizures along with a fever and vomiting. Medications were increased to help with the seizures. Doctors are saying his reflux is what needs to be controlled better, but those options are low. They are saying if he has to come back again with all of the same symptoms he will have to have surgery.

Nathaniel was released on Nov. 19th but we ended up back at Children's three days later and it was determined the surgery was needed to really change his way of life. The procedure is called a Nissen Fundoplication. It is the turning of the stomach, so when Nathaniel's reflux kicks in, the acid in his stomach has a harder route to travel up his esophagus and it will cut down on his vomiting so he can keep his nutrition in his body. He will have a Mic-Key button placed on his belly instead of that stupid G-Tube down his nose that was accidentally yanked out once and a while. Any operation Nathaniel has is a risky one because of his breathing and respiratory problems, but this is it, we must follow through with this operation, there is no way out. Nothing has worked and if this does not work it would only be a matter of time before we lose him if the seizures do not slow down or stop. We have been in the hospital since Nov. 22nd and it is time. The date was Dec. 15, 2002. Courtney and I talked to Nathaniel before he was taken to the operating room. A kiss and a hug from his big sister and mommy and a knuckle bump from dad. For the first time I started to think this could be the last time I could see him. I never thought that before. I have always realized he will never be like us and he will be constantly sick, but I never thought of losing him until now. He does not know the surroundings; he does not even know he is having surgery. He does know our voices, our shadows or images and our love. He just smiles as he leaves the room not knowing the seriousness of this procedure. He just knows his family's love.

Hours go by and I guess no news is good news. We then hear that he is OK but will be in recovery for a while. So I took Courtney home for a normal night and to get some sleep. Kim hung out until Nathaniel came back to his room. They wanted to perform a laparotomy with five little incisions, but to better the surgery the doctors decided to cut straight across his belly instead, about six inches long. The procedure was a success but he will need time to heal. I went back the next day and it was hard to see him this way. He could not be picked up and was really hurting from the surgery. He was on pain medication, but each time it would wear off and you could see and feel his pain. His cry was a painful cry not like the one's he had when he was born. Those cries were painful to me. I would try my best to console him. He would look towards me and had a look like, "Why does this hurt so much, daddy?" I felt helpless. I practically was climbing in bed with him for comfort. There was not much I could do. So we just cuddled.

I always talk about being in the wrong place at the wrong time, so this day I hung around for a long time and wanted to stay until he got his pain medication and got settled. I decide to make my trek home to beat that beltway traffic; come to think of it, there is no way of beating the beltway traffic. So I started out and about 10 minutes down the road I realize I had forgotten my wallet, which I left in the drawer of Nathaniel's night table. So I headed back. I get into his room and there are two Christmas bears in his bed. I thought how nice, those volunteers are always dropping off toys or stuffed animals for Nathaniel and Courtney when she is there.

Nathaniel's nurse walks in and says, "Did you get to meet her?" "Meet who?" I said. The nurse says "The First Lady!" I was like "What?" Then she says, "Yeah, she was just here and gave him a teddy bear. And the volunteer with her said Nathaniel has a big sister that is here with him a lot of the time. So the First Lady left a second bear for Courtney. I missed it all. My son gets to meet Laura Bush when I go and try to beat unbeatable traffic. Just my luck. The First Lady must have made a good impression on Nathaniel, he was settled and fast asleep. Or was it the drugs.

Nathaniel made it home for Christmas with his new Mic-Key button for feeding and he was digesting his food properly. Another cool thing was the doctors requested another eight hours of nursing at home and it was approved. So we set up a day nurse from 9:00 AM to 5 :00 PM for when I am at work. Being back at home, Nathaniel is feeling better, but one thing is really bothering him, he is seriously constipated. So back to urgent care we go and Nathaniel is put on liquid Colace. After two days, the flood gates opened and he was feeling more like himself.

In the New Year (2003) and the old saying, "The more things change, the more they stay the same." rings true for the Breen family. At least twice a month we were in the office of a specific doctor or we are in an emergency room between Frederick and Washington, D.C., or we are admitted for an overnight stay or two. And now something new has developed. Imagine that. One of Nathaniel's doctors would like to have a spinal x-ray done to evaluate what she thinks is a mild case of scoliosis with his spine. Could this be a start of something new? Why not, he seems to be getting everything else. The spring and summer were typical, a lot of chest congestion. Maryland's Early Intervention Program was a big help with all of the therapies. Each therapist would visit the house and get Nathaniel out of bed and moving. Physical and occupational therapies were performed on a weekly basis or sometimes monthly basis. Kim and I believe in every activity. We believe the stimulation is the best thing for him.

Something else that was stimulating around this time was the birth of Emma. A planned C-section went off without a hitch and the Breen family is a party of five. Well, with Nathaniel the way he is, it feels like a party of eight. Wait, cannot forget about mom and Pat. I say the more the merrier. When Kim and Emma came home for the first time, we laid Emma in Nathaniel's bed with him and he was wondering what the hell is this thing squirming around next to me. He was so curious and from the very first moment he seemed intrigued with who is this person smaller than me and crying, "why all of this crying?" I like to put quotation marks around some of Nathaniel's words because his eyes tell the words when the things I write about happen around him. He loves Emma. He loves the wonderment. You can see it on his face. You know he cares for Courtney and Emma. Man, this is going to be fun. And busy. Who cares? I love my family. With Emma home and Nathaniel interested in her and all of the repetitive nature of all of his therapies will make us hope that someday it will trigger Nathaniel's brain to remember to do these activities on showing signs of familiarity. The other reason this is so good for him, with the therapies, especially the physical therapy, we would love to keep him loose. I see a lot of children with Cerebral Palsy whose joints are so rigid and tight. It may be caused by the severity of their Cerebral Palsy or it has to do with the lack of attention parents give their children. I see it happen to Nathaniel if we miss a couple of sessions due to him being sick or a therapist misses a visit. You We must make an effort beyond your means to keep Nathaniel loose as a goose.

(October 9, 2003)

(We are seeing something different with Nathaniel now. He is laughing a lot. Sometimes it is uncontrollable and his whole body shakes. It seemed to be very refreshing to see this emotion from Nathaniel but when he gets too excited it starts to scare us. Sometimes we are ready to run him to the hospital. It seems to freak out Nathaniel, like he scares himself when it's over. What do we do now?)

Kim and I start out thinking this laughing is a great sign of emotion from Nathaniel. We video tape it to show off our man. But as the laughing starts, it is now becoming a bit uncontrollable along with his legs shaking and arms stiffening. It gets bad enough his lips start to turn blue. He is not taking any breaths. Now he is scaring us. We notice it more when he has a lack of sleep or he will get startled when something bangs loud. Then suddenly he is having seizures interrupting the laughing spells. We need to see a neurologist on a regular basis. So we get referred to one in Rockville, MD and things heat up.

(October 28, 2003)

(Today we are going to see a neurologist and hopefully we can make this a regular thing. The way Nathaniel's seizures change since he has been born, Kim says we need to have a neurologist on call. I agree. Maybe this person can figure Nathaniel out.)

Can someone help me get off the floor? I feel like I went through a 10-round fight with one arm tied behind my back and the other one trying to hold my head on straight. This lady beat the crap out of me, and I think we hit it off just fine. What did I just say? Maybe I hit my head on the floor before when I fell. I am talking about Nathaniel's new neurologist, Dr. Rajasingham. Nathaniel, his nurse and dad are headed down the road to Rockville, MD. We have not had a regular neurology appointment for a while, even though we have talked to them when we have been in the emergency room or when Nathaniel has been admitted. Maybe Dr. Rajasingham can be our regular neurological doctor. When we arrive of course, there is the mandatory paperwork, which takes about 35 minutes to fill out. We get called back for our appointment. As we get settled, my paperwork is still not finished. So Nathaniel's nurse gets him out of his kid cart, up on the exam table when suddenly the doctor comes in like a whirlwind. She excuses herself a couple of times to answer a phone call and to find paperwork on Nathaniel, which I still am working on and to find the paperwork from his regular doctor about his life history, which I still have in my hand. As she gets settled she says "What is the reason for your visit today?" I said; "To see you." She says; "Let me ask you again, what is the reason for your visit today?" I said, "Because of Nathaniel's seizures." She replied; "What seizures?" I said; "The seizures he is having constantly." This conversation goes on for a couple of minutes with the same type of questions. Then the original question is asked; "So what is the reason for your visit today?" I thought I was on a hidden camera show or something. Kim made the appointment so I thought it was clear the reason why we were there. So I made it more clearly by saying we have not seen a neurologist on a regular basis and we like to see if you can help us. For the first hour of this appointment, I felt like I was being interrogated with a bright light shining in my face. We were really butting heads. Then we decided to talk about Nathaniel's medical history. So I start from birth.

She stopped me every once and a while to ask me to elaborate on certain things. So for the second hour we relived Nathaniel's damaged life. I, of course, feel sad talking about Nathaniel in front of him. I feel guilty. You know how it is; you just do not talk about people in front of them especially when there is something wrong. It is uncomfortable for them and yourself. Dr. Rajasingham notices this is bothering me and she says "It's OK. I can tell he hears your voice and this comforts him." Now I start to feel comfortable around Dr. Rajasingham.

After examining Nathaniel she points out certain things and asks specific questions. Then she sits down, makes some notes, puts her pen down and says, "Are you ready?" I said, "Sure." She starts to tell me straight up, her honest, no blunt honest opinions and facts and what she thinks is really going on inside Nathaniel. I figure, finally, no sugar coating this day. She starts out with all of this information which I never thought of and how damaged he really is. At first it was like a left jab then a huge right hook, and then she planted one square on my chin. Down goes Breen! Down goes Breen! She floored me. And it hurt . . . emotionally. But, and this is a big but, it was what I wanted to hear for the past two almost three years of my son's life. Blunt, honest truth. She told me, "As much as Nate is a part of this family, like a son or daughter in any normal situation; he is what I call NOT NORMAL." For the rest of this appointment these words were thrown around the room very casually. I started to think of Nathaniel as ABNORMAL, in my mind he was just my son who was sick, not ABNORMAL. The truth does hurt.

What we tried to figure out this day was the frequency of Nathaniel's seizures and the spells of uncontrollable laughter, which is now considered seizure activity, and the lack of sleep he gets once a month for about three or four days in a row. What Dr. Rajasingham said next made me realize how to think about the way our family should and will live. She said, "Nathaniel has his own special way to deal with all of his obstacles and is totally different from the rest of the family." And as a mother and father, Kim and I have to resign ourselves to the fact this is the way it will always be with Nathaniel. She added, "As long as Nate's obstacles do not interfere with normal family life, let him be himself." I asked "How?" She replies, "If he only gets one hour of sleep in a 24 hour period, that's OK. If he is awake for two days, that's OK. Like I said before, if it does not upset the everyday activity of the rest of the family, let him be himself." She then went on to say, "This is why you have the nursing help. This is how his brain is going to function. He may not be able to think for himself but we cannot go crazy every time this happens." We must go on. When I first heard this I felt like we were leaving him behind, but we are not. For a long time this did upset our family life, but with the nursing and the adjustments of his medication we can deal better. Shit, Chris, the nurses will be there, use them to your advantage. Live with it. It will take a while to get the medications adjusted, but we now have a new rule to follow. It is so damn hard to swallow the truth about Nathaniel and what we have to do. We as a family must adjust our lives around Nathaniel and we have to let this grow on us.

(November 5, 2003)

(I feel more like a human these days. We are trying so hard with what Dr. Rajasingham has set for us. We are going to do more things together as a family. Unfortunately I mean Courtney, Emma, Kim and myself. When the weather is nice and Nathaniel is feeling good he will join us on our adventures.

He will need care for as long as he is alive. Weather permitting. I feel guilty leaving him home some times.)

I look at Nathaniel differently now. I sometimes refer to my every day activities as guilt. I feel guilty because I live my life playing games with Courtney and Emma and their friends, doing things together with Kim, even going to work. All of this in front of Nathaniel. These activities are normal activities. The guilt is felt because Nathaniel can do none of these things. The simplest of life's gifts are gone for Nathaniel. He needs Kim and me every day. Every moment he will be alive, he needs care. I come down stairs from a good night's sleep and I see Nathaniel with that deer-in-the-headlights look, eyes glazed over and very jumpy. I learn from the nurse he has only slept for 10 minutes. That's right only 10 minutes. No exaggeration. He seems exhausted but wide awake at the same time. Kim calls this "the look." The look of being awake but not there. A blank stare. No emotions. Can you see where our frustrations come from? He needs sleep, but how can we give it to him. I do not want to drug him with sleeping medicine or something like Valium all of the time. He deserves better.

Going into late fall and winter, again more of the same as last year. More congestion and colds are battled against. The seizures really act up we he is running a fever. Dr. Rajasingham has taken on Nathaniel as a regular patient, which has been a blessing. She really shows us the time and care we need with Nathaniel.

My work with Kim's aunt and uncle has been hard to handle. There has been no way for me to focus on any of my work. There is no motivation on my end. I have been just going through the motions and have not brought in any sales. Since graduating high school I have been in the floor covering business and the change for me has been difficult. I feel like I have let them down. My work ethic has struggled since the birth of Nathaniel. My concentration level is gone. All I think about is the struggle. I started to think of different ways to make money and just about invested money into starting an adult-natured website. Morally I knew it was wrong but my mind was going crazy trying to make money and get us out of this hole we have been in. In the end I knew it was wrong and decided to get back into the floor covering business. Kim and I appreciate everything they did for us and I am so very sorry for letting them down. They have helped us change our lives and gave us hope for a better future, for this I am forever grateful. We are also moving into a bigger house. Seven in a town house is tough. Now Nathaniel will have his own room on the first floor and not in a living room and dining room combo.

When late October rolls around there is a new obstacle for Nathaniel. A lot of kids with Cerebral Palsy sit frog legged. Since Nathaniel does this we suddenly start to hear him crying in pain. Not the consistent crying he used to have, you can tell it is pain. He was not moving his leg too much, and when we reposition him in bed, he would cry out loud. We always have to play the guessing game with Nathaniel because he cannot tell us where it hurts or what's wrong whenever something happens to him. We take him to get checked out and we find out that his hip is dislocated. With all of the things that can go wrong, this has to be the hardest. How are we to move him in this condition? He has to see an orthopedic doctor the next day so we have to take him home and then take him back out the next morning. This is a lot of moving. I know it is going to hurt him. So for the time being we are going to double diaper him. It was so hard to move him without hurting him. The two diapers were not a big help, he was in extreme pain each time we moved him. The doctor says he needs surgery as soon as possible. So we set up surgery a few days later on Oct.

25th. The doctor is going to insert a pin and plate on his hip and Nathaniel will be in a three-quarter body cast until he heals.

(October 26, 2004)

(Nathaniel is resting comfortably today. A cast from chest to toes. He looks uncomfortable. The pain medication is given every couple of hours to keep Nathaniel as comfortable as possible. I am now wondering how we are to handle him like this and how are we to get him home. Please God, help him heal all over. I don't know how much I can see him in so many predicaments.)

The hip was not the only thing fixed this day. Nathaniel also had an extra bone shaved down in his shoulder. Kim's side of the family has an extra bone syndrome called Osteochondroma where some bones grow hooks at the ends of them and can be sore if they grow too big or they grow too long, they can grab muscles or tendons. Kim has had a couple of surgeries to shave these bones down. Also, and add this to the growing list. Are you ready? We also receive word that after reviewing x-rays the doctor checked on Nathaniel's mild scoliosis, and it showed his spine is getting worse. So we decide to worry about that after we get Nathaniel healed. We get to visit him in recovery, when he is coming around we let him know we are here for him. We look under his warming blanket and see a body cast up to his chest. They cut a hole out for his feeding tube and around his butt so we can keep a diaper on him. He will be in this cast for at least eight weeks to let that joint heal.

Nathaniel, of course, comes through with flying colors, again. The one thing that concerns us about what the doctor said about his scoliosis was prevalent when he was in his cast. The cast was not perfectly straight around his chest area. You can feel his right side was tight against the cast. We check up on the scoliosis, and the doctor says his curvature was now about 53 degrees. More drastic than we expected. Of course, the remedy for the scoliosis is surgery. No! We cannot do this to him. What else can we do? How much more can he take? With surgery the doctors will install rods to straighten Nathaniel's spine and as he grows the rods will have to be adjusted. No! No! No! We cannot do this to him. The doctor asks if we would like a second opinion. So he sends us to see another orthopedic specialist. This doctor happens to be one of the best in the world and is well known. I was working, so Kim and Nathaniel's nurse Terry and the girls took Nathaniel to the appointment. Kim called me after the appointment and was very upset. I asked her what happened. She said the doctor came in very arrogant, full of self-importance like his shit did not stink, checks Nathaniel's x-rays, looks at Nathaniel (no interaction, of course) and says he will set a date for surgery. Kim said, "Hi, I am Kim Breen and this is Nathaniel. Who said we were going to have surgery? We wanted your opinion on what to expect if we decide to have surgery or what other things can we consider, like braces?" The doctor says, "He must have surgery, he needs it." Well Kim and I have thought this over and do not like the idea of surgery. If we go on and decide to operate, first of all any surgery is risky for Nathaniel because of his breathing issues. Then we are talking about the spine, there is a chance of paralysis. We are also talking about surgery on a child who cannot and will never walk, crawl, sit up on his own and do any activity at all, just lay there in a hospital bed (and we do not leave him there all of the time). Basically he is paralyzed and he cannot do anything without our help. Surgery also means pain. He will be doped up consistently for that pain and as he grows further surgeries will be needed to extend the rods. So Kim tells the doctor we have already decided not to go through with this surgery. The doctor packed up Nathaniel's file says, "Fine" and walks out of the room. Kim did not know if he was coming back to help with options or he was done with the appointment. The nurse walks in and asks Kim and Terry if they need help packing up. The two of them looked at each other like "did this just happen?" That jackass was done with Kim and said absolutely nothing. She wanted to talk but he had no time for us and Nathaniel if he was not going to operate. Kim tells me this and I go through the roof. We are asking for help. If the surgery is the only option, tell us. We are not the experts here, isn't he? So I think. When I get home from work, I call and leave a message for him to call us back and maybe he could give us some ideas on what we can do since we decided not to have the surgery. Two days later, and no it was not the weekend, a nurse calls from his office and says, "Maybe some braces will slow his scoliosis down but they will not stop it." So I asked if I could talk to the doctor, I think he owes us that much. She says no. I said, "His bedside manor sucks!" "Just because he was featured on TV about his skills and what obstacle he had to overcome, doesn't mean he can pick and choose who he talks too or walks out on." We have been through hell and back and we don't need assholes like him walking out on my son when we were asking for help, we had enough of that in other places. By the time I was done ranting, the nurse asked me not to call the office again. "Good!" I said. "And you make sure to pass every word along to him." I think before I get that out of my mouth, she hung up on me. Oh well, I am interested in quality of life for my son, I don't have time for people who don't have time for us.

Kim and I have weighed the options and turned to our relatives and friends and asked their opinions of surgery or no surgery, and we all believe to let Nathaniel be himself. The quality of life in either circumstance is not great, but I could not put him through another long process of surgery and recovery with other surgeries down the road. And I fully understand if we let his scoliosis go on, the curvature could start affecting his vital organs. If he could walk or crawl, I would have no doubt about surgery, but to have it so he could lay straighter in his hospital bed for longer periods of time and go through it later, over and over. No thanks. Yes, I understand the good things about making life manageable for anyone. The surgery could help, but when was the last time you met or heard someone who had back surgery with rods inserted and everything went well with no complications or no more severe back pain. Everyone I have met (five or six people) regret having the surgery, every single one of them. I think we will have him just the way he is now. Every decision we make, deals with life or death for Nathaniel. I cannot believe we have to do this on a regular basis. I know there are other families out there like ours and even in worse situations, I just cannot believe this mess and how the hell do we get out of it. Well, I have come to the conclusion, we don't. We just deal with it.

As another year comes to an end, things are cool. Having Emma around has been so rewarding. She is the part of Nathaniel we didn't get. She runs the house. She runs all over Nathaniel and he loves the rough stuff. When Courtney and Emma and their friends are playing around Nathaniel, we can see his face light up and he kicks his legs like he wants to get up and run around with them, unfortunately that will not happen, but we make due. We put him down where the action is and he loves every minute of it. We try to make every situation as normal as possible. After Nathaniel turned three, he got to go to school at the Rock Creek School here in Frederick. The bus picks him up in front of the house and he goes to school for a half a day, five days a week. He gets all of the therapies and attention he received with the Early Intervention Program. The unfortunate thing is a lot of these kids go to school sick and in Nathaniel's atmosphere he will catch what they have very easily. So school is not a full-time adventure yet.

Nathaniel's day nurse Terry picks up the pieces when he cannot go to school. Terry has been a godsend. I kid with her after she told me her hands have been touched by God a long time ago. She is blessed, I believe. She gives Nathaniel all of her spirit to survive day to day. She is Nathaniel's right hand girl. She gets him started every day she is here. He sometimes rolls his eyes like "Is she here again?" But without her caring heart and those touched hands Nathaniel would not be who he is today. She is loud, she is rough and she gets him to come out of his shell every day. And he plays right along with her. Terry does all of the range of motion exercises and gets him up and moving if he likes it or not. She will not let him take a step or two back. Terry will do all of the same things at the same times every day to give Nathaniel some normalcy in his life. And he responds to it. Even though Terry is a New York Yankees homer, we love her dearly and she is part of our family forever. She says she will be his nurse for as long as he can stand her. What Terry doesn't know is that Nathaniel has her under his spell when he bats those long eyelashes at her. She cannot resist. No one can resist him. He has a loving way about him and he doesn't even know it. And you know why he has that loving way, because we show him nothing but love. He knows no other way. He may have a fever of 103 degrees and will still smile at you. How does he go through all of this shit he goes through and smile? That is just Nathaniel doing what he does best. I tell him to keep it, boy, and you will go places. I know the one place he goes consistently, is to everyone's heart.

This chapter covered a couple of long years of a very sick child's life. Things have been crazy, but we push onward but not upward. We struggle financially, as I suspect families do in our shoes. Most of Nathaniel's stuff is covered by the state of Maryland, but at some point they want to get paid. We are constantly searching the internet on our faulty computer for ideas on how to get everything Nathaniel deserves. But when you find some things that will help, you get discouraged with all of the mounting paperwork. We must go on with our lives, there has to be a way to make life easier and less hectic. It does take a toll on us, physically and emotionally.

Kim and I balance each other out a lot of the time, but there are times we look at each other and think "what's next?". I know what's next, how would you like to meet my beautiful wife. Kimberly is the rock this family is built on. See how she does it. Just ask Nathaniel, he is a momma's boy.

CHAPTER IV

Kim: A Heavenly Angel In Training

Since our very first date, I knew Kimberly was the girl for me because we hit it right off. So many things were right about us, it was scary. I never really thought of Kim as the one I am going to settle down with. What I always thought, and still do today, I think of Kim as my life. She came into my life. She became my life and she is my life everlasting.

What you are about to read is my tribute to Kimberly. Not just facts and opinions about her but my inner most feelings will be shown. My thoughts, her thoughts, they are all the same. Our compatibility is off the charts. We have been to the end of our ropes many a time, but one of us has always pulled the other one back. When I look into her eyes I see the passion, I see her unselfishness in life. As many problems as we have no one can say they see it in our actions. We try to go about life as if none of this ever happened to Nathaniel or we try to keep it as simple as possible. I know a lot husband and wives' who would have crumbled, believe me, I have seen it all too often. But not us, we just fell more in love. It is our nature to keep plugging along. Yeah, sure, we have had a horrible time figuring out what to do for Nathaniel from day one and yeah we have cried our eyes out for him but in the long run, it has made us stronger on the inside. We didn't mess this up, other people screwed up, but sometimes we fall into this trap of guilt. I still do, maybe Kim does at times but the past is just that, the past. Yeah it hurts us but we must focus on life at hand and the future. Two beautiful girls depend on us for our help. If I could pick one moment in time when my wife's love shined the brightest was on the day she was coming home from the hospital after Nathaniel was born.

Before we left, we were told we could hold Nathaniel for the first time. Sort of like a consolation prize. Kim jumped at the opportunity to hold him, she was so excited. So we scrubbed up, I had the video camera ready and in we went. It took a nurse and a doctor about 10 minutes to get Nathaniel from his bed to Kim's arms in the rocking chair. They were trying to figure out how to give him to Kim with all of the wires and tubes. I was already taping our big event. I was watching Kim's face and it was full of excitement but as the minutes went on, you could see her expression change to a sad look. They finally passed Nathaniel to Kim and they straightened all of the tubes and wires and get him settled, as they moved from in front of me I finally get a shot of my wife and son together for the first time. I noticed something beautiful through the video camera. There is something quite magical when a mother holds her son for the first time. Kim had a glow about her. The worried look in her eyes was gone and it was replaced with a warm peaceful stare at her son. And you could tell Nathaniel knew who was holding him. She talked to him in her softest voice and he started to open his eyes but this cruel world was too bright. Kim said it was great to feel him squirm in her arms. It was sad not being able to hear him yet because of the ventilation tube down his throat, but seeing mommy hold him made our day.

Kim has the gentlest demeanor of anyone I have ever met. She will lend a helping hand to anyone who needs it. Throughout every summer, Kim will watch our friend's kids so our friends do not have to pay for camp or babysitters. She doesn't skip a beat. You would never know all of the shit she has gone through by the way she goes about everyday life. Along with everything that has gone wrong with Nathaniel, Kim, like everyone else has her own ailments and they are more drastic than you think. She has Crohn's Disease. An intestinal disorder where Kim has a seemingly endless cycle of flare-ups of upset stomach and diarrhea and the most severe episodes of intestinal blockages. This at times can cause her to have surgery for the blockages. She has had two resection surgeries already and has been on steroids and countless medications to fight this devastating disease. She battles with the Crohn's every day. It will make Kim miss social activities and family events. I myself have missed work frequently over the years either because of Kim getting sick with her Crohn's or Nathaniel's Cerebral Palsy and seizures, and I believe it will be a never-ending battle of health. But no matter what she goes through, others come first in Kim's world.

She never puts herself first, I am constantly telling her to go out and play bingo or sit at the local coffee shop and read a book. Since I work, Kim does the load of work for Nathaniel every day. She is constantly on the phone with a coordinator, nursing agency or even calling in prescriptions. You name it; she is on the phone keeping everyone else on the same page. All the while raising Courtney and Emma. As the girls are getting older; there are more places they must be. We are already seeing that in Courtney. She has to be doing something all the waking day. Courtney wants to have three friends over and be at four friends' houses at the same time. Emma is no longer the tag along, but soon will be just as busy as Courtney. Kim and I look at the girls, they deserve better. Always. We try to make everyday life as simple as possible. The more friends that are over, the better.

For Courtney's eighth birthday party, she asked Kim to have a slumber party. So Kim asked me and I thought it was a great idea. What I agreed to next should have made me eligible for either the Father Hall of Fame or committed to an insane asylum. I let Kim go out to bingo that night, forgetting that there is a slumber party that night with nine girls watching the premiere of High School Musical 2. This means it is four hours of "What the hell was I thinking?" Nathaniel wasn't even on my side, with all of the craziness of the slumber party; Nathaniel decides to have one of his biggest bowel movements on record. The only good thing about this bowel movement was that the smell cleared the girls out and up to Courtney's room so my brain could clear. But you know what; I would not have it any other way. Seeing the smiles on the girls' faces means mommy and daddy are doing the right things. The most important thing this night also gave Kim a well-deserved break and a night to unwind. By the way, Kim won $250.00 at bingo. I asked for the money as my fee for being super dad. I was denied my request. Girls still rule this house. I always say at least Nathaniel is on my side, you know us men stick together. Then Kim reminds me he is a momma's boy, so I still lose. So she thinks.

Speaking of being a momma's boy, Nathaniel always lights up when Kim walks into the room. Seeing the bond between them truly makes my heart happy. It is a bond that I see that Nathaniel shines the most. I could be in the room for an hour playing and talking to him, and I must say I get a great reaction out of him, but when mommy walks in the room and says one word, his head will snap around in her direction. Kim gets the most out of him. When she talks to him, his level of concentration is remarkable. I do believe when a child is in the womb, he or she can hear what is going on in the outside world and this is where Nathaniel makes his first connection with his mommy. Even through all of the shit that went on at birth, I believe he knows mommy the best, and that is why he reacts the way he does. She shows Nathaniel nothing but love.

When couples decide to start a family, they take a leap of faith, love and hope together. Kim and I leaped head first into parenting when Kim gave birth to Courtney within our first year of marriage. Kim seemed to slip right into her role as a mother. Dad, on the other hand, I was scared shitless. If Kim was scared, she sure did not show it. She was confident in every move she made; it really came natural for her. I was a very proud father, but when I first started to carry Courtney, I would carry her as if I was carrying a ticking bomb about to explode. But as I watch Kim, I learned to let Courtney melt into my arms and body. And soon I became one with Courtney. She has taught me to be the man, husband and father I am today. My focus was changed shortly after the birth of Courtney. We were no longer just husband and wife, we are now a family. Kim's nurturing of Courtney looked so natural and the rest just rubbed off on me. I became more motivated as a father, especially when I realized I can do more things with Courtney on my own. I enjoyed going over my mom's house and showing Courtney off. I even loved to go to the mall. Now that scares me.

When we found out we were pregnant with Nathaniel, I was getting more excited to step up and be a father. But with all of the shit that happened at the birth of Nathaniel, Kim really went to the front of the line of motherhood. She was now a part of the fraternity of mothers in this world with a disabled child. This is where her heavenly angel-in-training began. From the moment Kim held Nathaniel, she knew things were going to be different and her level of mothering would have to be raised. The most remarkable thing I noticed was how calm Kim was as she juggled Courtney and Nathaniel's needs flawlessly. We both dig deep into our souls every time to get past every obstacle imaginable with Nathaniel. I have watched her closely since Nathaniel's birth and I have seen her transform into a woman on a mission to keep her son alive and well. Never once have I seen her give up on her mission. She is constantly keeping all of Nathaniel's entities in line. He needs these people for his welfare. She tirelessly tries new avenues of help for Nathaniel. We both believe there is something out there we have not tried or seen that will help make Nathaniel better or more comfortable.

When Emma came along, Kim really had her hands full when I was at work. Emma was moving fast. Crawling and walking at an early age and she was always into something that she should not get into. Kim really wanted to see the interaction with a third child, boy or girl, with Nathaniel. We did not want what happened to Nathaniel stop us from having a third child. The love and reactions from Emma towards Nathaniel are outstanding. She climbs all over him and he loves it. He wonders what the hell is going on but he loves it. With all that goes on, our friends and relatives say, in their house you would have no idea there is something different about them. And we like to keep it that way. Courtney and Emma have every right and chance to be free of Nathaniel's disability. We do not want them to feel burdened with all that mommy and daddy have to handle. Sometimes the two do cross over and Courtney and Emma understand. They might not be happy, but they understand.

During the summer time, Kim keeps the girls and their friends busy with arts and crafts, trips to Greenbrier State Park where there is a beach area, to the wooden slide the Amish built in Thurmont, MD, movies, and the mall when it is too hot outside. Kim is non-stop. As dad, I am the relief pitcher when I come from work. I try to give Kim as many breaks as possible. Yes, we still do have nursing, but when I come home, we are as normal a family as we can be. This coming year, school is for all of our kids. Emma will be in pre-kindergarten, Courtney will be in third grade and Nathaniel will be heading back to Rock Creek School, but now we have permission to keep him home. Nathaniel gets the colds and what everything else the kids bring to school very easily because of his respiratory condition. This means Kim will have some mommy time to herself for a little while. Kim needs this time for herself. Same with daddy, but Kim needs this more than I do. Along with the challenges of Nathaniel, the running around with Courtney and Emma and the phone glued to her ear, she has the Crohn's disease to deal with of her own.

Kim has had Crohn's since she was young, but was never diagnosed with it until she was in the Army. "Army?" Never would have pegged her for an Army girl when I met her. She told me, growing up she had to earn the respect of her elders (I know that all too well) and of course, earn a living. When she ran out of money to finish up college she decided to join the Army. Still that surprises the hell out of me. After joining, she received her basic training at Fort Dix in New Jersey. Then she was stationed at Fort Hood in Texas. She even spent time at Camp Darby in Italy. All of this within three years. Her time in the Army was cut short. She was getting sick a lot and not able to keep food down. I used to hear Army food would do that to you but this was very different. She was given an appointment to get some X-rays. When something was spotted, she was then given a colonoscopy. She had developed some severe blockage in her lower intestine, which was finally diagnosed as Crohn's Disease, which is when the intestines do not digest her food properly or the intestines are lined with ulcers that flare up when food passes through and causes a blockage. Kim was told she needs surgery to remove a part of her intestines that has the blockage and then resect the intestines back together.

She ended up in the hospital for five months after the surgery fighting off fevers and infections. Since then she has had multiple episodes of bloating and blockages that has led to one surgery after another since we have been married. I was scared for Kim. I know any surgery is risky but messing around with the stomach and intestines are tricky. It messes with your eating, your digesting of food, your ability to break down your nutrients, the way you live day to day. Then she has to put up with me. Remember I had my car accident when we first moved to Maryland, then I wanted to get that rod out of my leg, so there is another surgery. Then in January of 2006 I dislocated and broke my ankle in three places playing ice hockey, don't ask. I will fill you in later. I needed surgery to fix two of the three breaks. We are sure messed up. Kim just stopped smoking and I am over weight. We now have to do something for not just the children, but for ourselves.

From time to time, Kim gets these feelings, and when she does, things happen. Take, for instance, the night we met. I thought I blew it. My friend Mike and my sister Kathy and I were out at a club to see my other friends' band the night before Thanksgiving. We were dancing on the dance floor next to Kim and her friend Alice so we all started to dance together. Of course, I liked her from the moment I saw her but I had a problem telling her so. You know, shy. So a little later, I excused myself to go to the men's room. I asked Kim to hold my frosty beverage of choice. When in the bathroom, I met a longtime friend I had not seen in a while. Anthony Manci, "Manc" for short, who I played hockey with some three years back. He informed me the team is getting back together and they were trying to figure out how to get a hold of me to play goalie. I said, "I'm in!" Then I thought, "I'm in alright, I'm in trouble!" I suddenly realized I was talking to "Manc" for at least twenty minutes. So I excused myself and went back to where Kim and everyone were at and there she was, holding my frosty beverage. Well, a non-frosty beverage, but she was still holding it. I thought, "This is the girl for me." I kiddingly tell that story to anyone who will listen, and now you all know, so Kim will be glad I don't have to tell that corny story any more. She had every right to dump that drink over my when I returned, but that is not Kim. She is the most level-headed person I know. I tried to propose marriage to her in the same spot we met, but she saw me through hundreds of people coming through the front door, about 150 feet away and part way around a corner. She had one of those feelings again.

Back to present day, our lives are upside down. We hardly ever get to go out together, but when we do, we try to enjoy every moment of it. If there is one thing in our lives I wish we had more of is time together. We do so many things separately it sucks. We make the time, but more is always needed. When we do go out, we are usually exhausted. People ask us how we do it all of the time and our answer always is "you have too." Our climate is at a higher level. You must adjust emotionally and physically to your life day after day. When we bounce off walls it does not hurt as much. Our bumps and bruises are just tough skin now.

Kim endures more than I do. Well, look, it is hard not to. She has those female issues every month, she has the Crohn's Disease, and she has the extra bones. But she goes through with everything without losing her faith and love. She always has the hope of an easier life for her girls and the comfort for her son. And she has a loving husband who will be at her side forever. Kim makes the hardest things seem simple. Every challenge has its ups and downs, but she focuses on the ups and makes them work. The effort is always there. She puts forward the time and sees it all the way through, no matter how exhausting it may be when it comes to the family, it has to get done. Even in her relaxing times, her mind is constantly on the girls and Nathaniel.

Just the other day on my day off, we were helping the girls clean their rooms and Kim walked into Emma's room and hands me a piece of paper from Courtney's room. They love playing school with their friends and it looks like Courtney was pretending to do a homework assignment and she wrote, "My life is different than some peoples. Like some people are rich and some people are poor. And some people cannot even have their own houses, THE END." It made us sad. We thought she was talking about us. We are constantly battling with debt and medical bills; we always make sure we pay what is needed every month. It is hard for me to keep a job that pays really well or I run into asshole employers that do not get what I have to do day in and day out. Not long ago Kim had an episode where she was misdiagnosed a couple of times and ended up in two different hospitals three times in three weeks. I just cannot put the kids in a day care. With what money? And who would take care of Nathaniel if there were no nurses available? Kim finally comes home and three days later, she calls me at work and tells me she is going to call 911 for Nathaniel because he was having seizure after seizure and his heart was racing to 170 beats per minute and a fever that spiked to 103 degrees. So again, I have to leave. So I really have to search for jobs that are not a big deal or the owners understand my situation. I cannot work sales, especially commission sales where I need to work fifteen 15 hours a day to make any money. So when you think of it, Nathaniel's unfortunate accident has caused us major financial trouble day to day. Seeing Courtney write something like she did means she knows all too well what is going on.

She is a very bright young girl who really follows in her mom's footsteps. She sees our struggles and she hears our tone when we are desperate for help. Kim says over and over she does not want all of this to fall on the girls' shoulders. Like I always say, the girls deserve better. They don't need to see or hear our struggles as they grow. We want them to be free spirited girls who love their brother and do not think of him as he is the one holding them back. That is why Kim keeps them busy like nothing ever happened to Nathaniel. And Kim really gets the girls to interact with their brother. And Nathaniel loves it. He knows his sisters. I do not know how he knows, but mommy pounds it into him every day.

Kim's angel training comes to her pretty easy. She works hard and it mostly works out naturally. Her gentle touch and her loving patience have paid off. Because she is a mom. She gives her all every day. I probably repeated some of these lines a couple of times throughout this chapter and book, and I do not want to use every single cliché to describe my wife. I just want people to understand, when it came down to it, my wife stood up higher than ever before. She has put her life on hold to take care of her son. She will never give in and let her son become a statistic. She works with and plays with her girls like nothing drastic ever happened to Nathaniel or harp on his injuries, and she makes sure the girls enjoy their young lives. She loves her husband and is glad she had one of her "feelings" when we first met. She also knows I will be here for her whenever she needs a laugh or a shoulder to cry on.

Of course, if there is one thing to trade in life it would be what happened to Nathaniel, but as another cliché goes, "If life gives you lemons, you make lemonade." Well, we were given Nathaniel and we are still making a beautiful family.

If I were allowed only one thing to say about my loving wife, it would be this: Kim is the rock on which this family is built on. I am no slouch myself, but Kim is US. Kim is mommy, wife, and heavenly angel in training. No matter what happens in the future, Kim, you have already earned your wings.

I Love You!

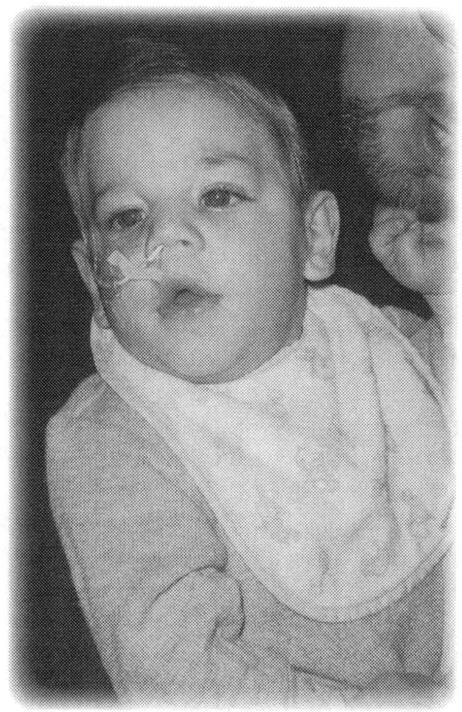

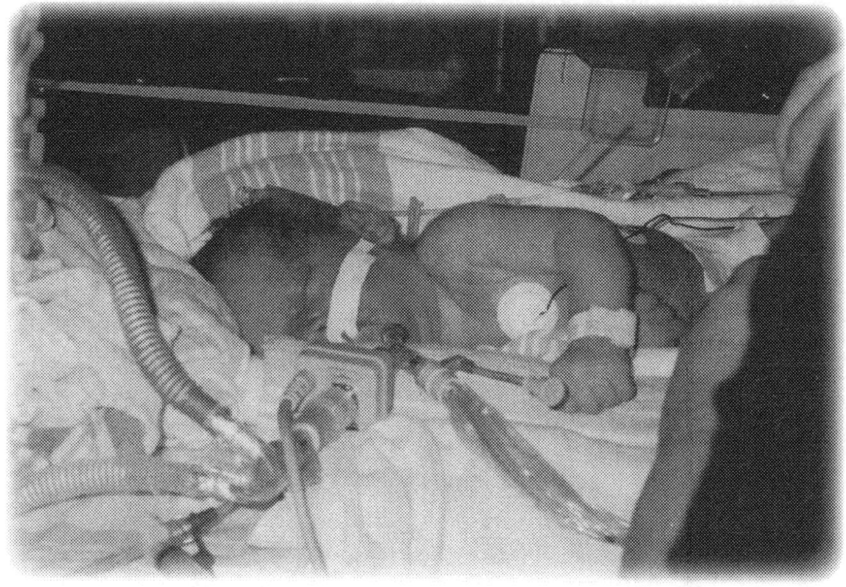

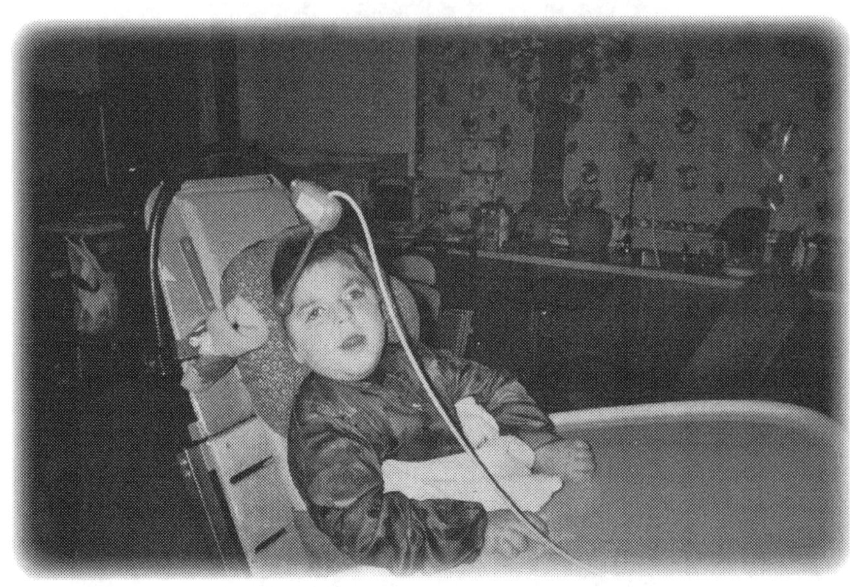

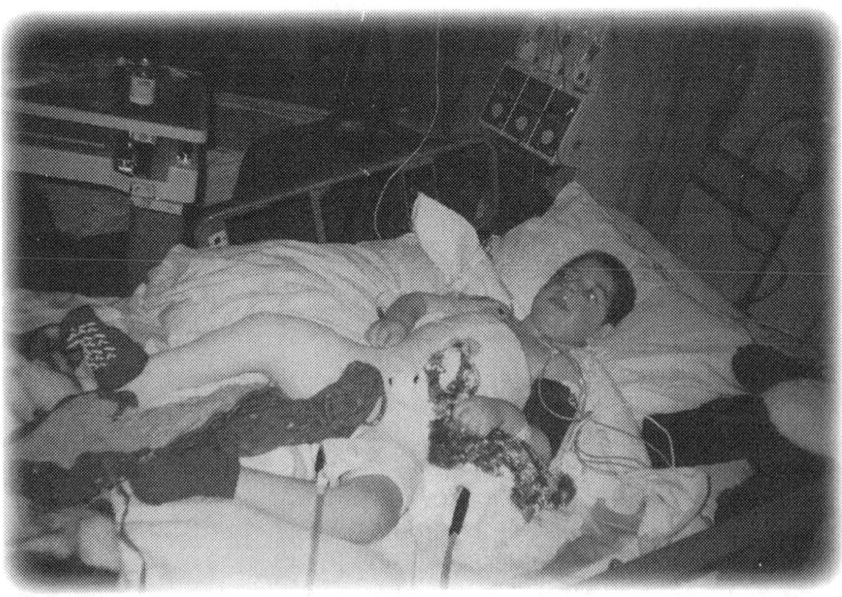

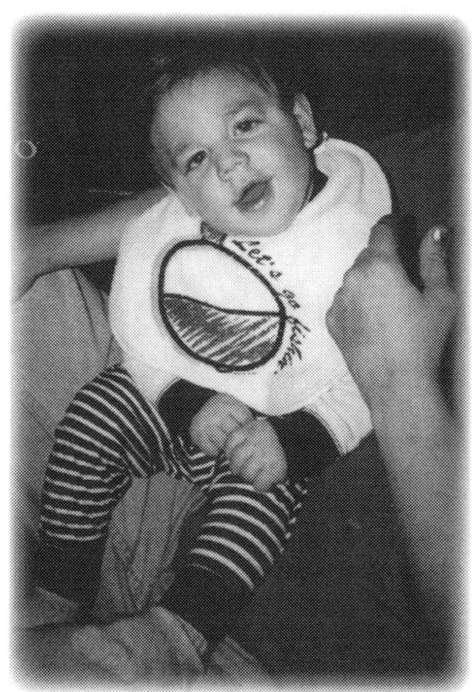

CHAPTER V

"Down And Out!" No! No! No! . . . settling Down And Figuring It Out!

After Nathaniel's visit to the stuck up, "how dare you question my genius mind" orthopedic surgeon, Kim and I were so fed up, and we decided to kick back and thought it's time to have a party. A party to celebrate our son. Listen, with all of the things that can go wrong having the surgery, there are things that could go wrong without having the surgery. The curvature of the spine could start to affect some of Nathaniel's vital organs. Heart, lungs, liver. It all could turn into only a matter of time. We'd rather have him go out on his own terms, not another medical procedure. But when we thought of it, it was a lack of medical attention that got Nathaniel into all of this shit in the first place.

So on that note, let us celebrate the young man who has been through so much in such a short time. We invite everyone. Family, friends, nurses and teachers. Our main reason is to explain what is going on with Nathaniel and what our course of action will be. We want everyone to understand the decision we have made and why we are going through with it. Nathaniel has been through the ringer. He does not need something to help him get around. He cannot walk, crawl, or even roll over and he never will without assistance. At this point, I do not know what the others will think, I hope they understand. I never thought we would be in a position like this one. The decision we have made was hard and easy. It plays so much on our mind, we just want to scream. Are we really going to let this to go on? Every time I reassure myself we are going in the right direction, I think of the future consequences of our action.

So we go on with the party to celebrate Nathaniel and we gather everyone together and tell them what is going on and what we have decided to do. Everyone agrees. They ask us if we have weighed all of the options, and we say yes over and over. So they back us up. Some say they cannot imagine what we are feeling and how we are dealing with such a situation. Kim and I tell them we cannot be selfish. We of course wanted Nathaniel to be normal, but that cannot happen. So we look to the next best thing. Being comfortable. This is all we can ask for. Nathaniel's mannerisms have always been smiles and that is the way we want him, nothing but smiles. On the day celebrating his life, Nathaniel was on his game. He was so happy. A full night of sleep and a bath with dad in the Jacuzzi tub. We were smelling like manly men. We dressed like manly men and we looked like manly men. I admit it, I love introducing Nathaniel to everyone. He deserves the spotlight. A lot was stolen from him when he was born and we want him to enjoy every day life as normal as possible just like his sisters.

As the party begins, I put up a framed picture that I made earlier in the week for everyone to see. It was a saying Kim and I read and then added to it. When I first saw it, it was Nathaniel. The words fit his life perfectly and the rest I added was from Kim and myself. It read:

> Nathaniel, never let anyone tell you the word CAN'T.
> Nathaniel CAN'T sit alone, but who wants too.
> Nathaniel CAN'T stand alone, but who needs too.
> Nathaniel CAN'T speak our language, but is understood.
> What Nathaniel CAN DO is melt anger with a smile.
> Nathaniel CAN quiet a room without speaking.
> Nathaniel has the right to be happy and comfortable.
>
> And Nathaniel can teach every one of us that the little things are what are important.
>
> Nathaniel is our gift and we are forever grateful to have him in our lives.
>
> Love,
> Mommy and Daddy

When it was read, everyone agreed it was Nathaniel. Of course, with all of his prep work to be a manly man, he decides to take a long nap during the whole party. But everyone enjoyed his company anyway.

(January 12, 2005)

(My mind feels at ease tonight. We just had a party for Nathaniel and it really seems everyone is on our side about our decision about not having the surgery. At least no one said anything about it aloud. It is just another weight off our shoulders, I hope we are right.)

Now I am back to feeling like we live in constant fear of Nathaniel catching the simplest of colds, which could lead into a battle for his life. You can try not to dwell on it but is stays in the back of your mind. You may put it out there that this is a pretty drastic thing to say, but it is true. If we do not stay one-step ahead of a cold, it could turn into a sinus infection or he can aspirate with all of the mucus in his chest and lungs and then that could turn up as pneumonia. So we still juggle with whether we can go out as a family or is it too cold or too humid.

Nathaniel had a great couple of weeks before Halloween, so we decide to get a costume for him and go trick or treating. He is a puppy dog this year. Emma is a ladybug, Courtney is a lady devil in a red dress and daddy, of course, is Winnie the Pooh. A six-foot Pooh. To some children, a scary site. Halloween night is a nice night, so we venture throughout the neighborhood and Nathaniel was stiff as a board in his wheelchair, full of excitement. He even gave himself a short seizure. I was a proud father with my kids. All three of them were having a great time. All of the sudden, I felt myself step back for a moment to just soak it all in and a tear came to my eye when I said to myself, "This is the meaning of life!" To watch my children experience life as it happens. To have them go through those feelings I had doing the same thing I did some years earlier. I hope my girls step back when they are older and get the warm feeling I have at this moment. Or maybe it is because I am in this Winnie the Pooh costume. The joke I heard that night and every Halloween I wear the costume is "Who did you lose a bet too?" My response is always "I do it for my kids!"

Nathaniel will never be able to reciprocate my love for him. How hard do you think it is to have your son not be able to function in ALL of the essential needs of a full life? As I go on with my life, I constantly remind myself or remind Courtney and Emma when they complain about doing chores, that Nathaniel can do none of these things we do day to day. I catch myself the majority of the day coming back to him. My emotions are always running rampant. Am I finding out why I am here now? Maybe God has given Kim and me a mission to complete, but why is Nathaniel the chosen one to be hurt? He did nothing to deserve this shit! What is his meaning? Was it to test us as parents? Well, if it is a test, how do I know I am passing? What do I have to do to get back in the good graces of God?

The whole family went back to church recently and the message being taught this day was Stress, Fracture. When I saw the sign, it made me laugh. This was going to be right up our alley. The lesson was about letting God hear me. We were given an example from the movie The Apostle where the star Robert Duvall is in his bedroom one night asking God why is he having so much trouble with his preaching's and his acceptance of him by other people. He is really letting God have it and wants his answer right now. This took me back in time, this was me in the hospital chapel, laying in my own vomit, I was really letting God have it too, and I wanted my answer right then and there.

I watch and listen to so many different ways people cope, the way they vent and the way they analyze the lives of others. They all have their degrees and they lecture on what's made them the expert they are today. But, why can't I do this, I am living it. I figure I can spread my word on how Kim and I have made it work. Giving our personal incite on how to cope and how you have to reach deep into the core of your soul and pull out the goodness and the needed patience to be a willing participant in your son's or daughter's lives, disabled or not.

But then you have to reach deeper. Put away petty things, put away your angst. You have to know it is not just for you, it is for the nurturing of a child. Yeah, I know we have a lot to do every day but make the time to be relevant. Do not just go through the motions. Make sure you widen your attention span and listen to your kids. I mean really listen. They have this great way of telling their stories of their young lives. Cherish those stories; see how they interpret life as we know it. I bet you can take yourself back in time to when you were a kid and things were simple. See the passion in their eyes when they accomplish something, and give you that look of; "I did it!"

Let's get back to the basics. The simplest of all is RESPECT. I believe we have lost this most important meaning of our lives. When I was growing up, if you did not respect each other or respect lessons handed down to you, you were knocked upside your head. We need to recapture this way of life. Respect is not just given to you, you need to earn it! Build character with the raw purpose to make things better for all of us. If you don't do things like this for your kids or you are not active in their lives, you are not a father. You know who you are out there. The men, I mean non-men, who sit there idle while their child suffers, get off your ass and get involved. Make an attempt to be a father.

Since joining the fraternity of fathers with kids with disabilities, the one unfortunate thing I have noticed is the lack of them. I have met or seen too many single mothers with these children. I know it is hard but you must take some responsibility, please? We live next to a couple who have a daughter who is a single mom with a child with Cerebral Palsy. He is 9 years old with no father figure around except for grand pop. This is not how it is supposed to be, come on. If you learn that your child has problems like Cerebral Palsy or something as difficult, step up to the plate. It will make you more of man than you can imagine. The fathers I do know, all have a special vibe about them. All of their kids no matter how damaged they are, they light up when daddy walks into the room. So if you think you cannot "deal", which I had to learn to do, you must dig deeper into your soul and find the way to make your child feel like they are wanted and loved. To be a father is a gift that you chose to become as you let human nature take its course. If you think your work is too busy or too important and this child could only interfere, keep your penis in your pants from now on, we do not need your donation to society any longer. This goes for you dads who do not have disabled children also. If you are not going to be a willing participant in the lives of your future children, keep it in your pants. And dads, if you are thinking of walking away because it is too hard, suck it up and make it work out. If you have a disabled child, think of their injury, their life is hard from the very beginning. They are the ones suffering, not you. Don't forget your kids! Do not use them as leverage against your spouse. If you turn your back on them, they could do the same to their children and so on and so on for generations to come. This is becoming an epidemic in our country and around the world. Learn to keep your focus on the lives of your children, I did. It was extremely hard when Nathaniel came along and it took all I have to figure it out. Come to think of it, I still struggle on how to figure things out. There are so many variables that go into making decisions in life, either it be for yourself or a loved one. When it is a loved one, in my case, Nathaniel, you are changing the course of a life. Not just his, but everyone around him. But try is what I am doing. Step back for a moment, watch your children and realize what they are experiencing, life will become a whole lot clearer when you see the joy in your children's eyes. Listen, I have no degrees and I am certainly no expert, nor do I claim to be one, I have found the understanding of my purpose as a father. But where did it come from?

The memories of my dad are in me, but a lot of them are fuzzy at best. He passed away when I was 9 years old, so I never really got to know him like my older brothers and sisters. Even from the age of 7 I did not get to see much of him, he was in and out of the hospital so much and he became so frail I didn't even recognize him. When he was home he stayed in his bedroom most of the time. When he did feel better we had this big orange pleather lounger with a gigantic wooden handle on the side which took out a shin or two in its day, and this thing would recline to a position so low it was damn near impossible to get out of it. It sat right in the middle of my bedroom along with two twin beds and queen size bed on the other side of the room. When dad felt well enough to get up, he sat in the lounger and this is when I had some time with him. We would catch a show or two, but not much was said. I knew he was sick but I had no idea how bad.

I never felt I got much from him. No real life lessons or a one-on-one sit downs. I just felt as if we past each other. Don't get me wrong, there was father/son interaction, but most of it I have no recollection because I was so young. As I was growing up I started to feel cheated, but I was surrounded by women (mom, Pat, Anna and grand mom) who showed me the way. I never asked what kind of man my dad was, so a couple of months ago I asked my brothers and sisters for some of their memories of dad. I thought maybe I could find out through them who dad was as a father to them, a husband to my mom and a man among his peers. What I found out next shocked me.

My sister Theresa told me one of her earliest memories of dad was when she was around 5 years old. She would hear dad get up for work every morning at five. Her bed was up against the wall in her room which connected to the bathroom. She would have to use the bathroom every time she woke up at that time. Theresa would knock on the door and dad would always step out into the hallway and let Theresa do her thing. When she finished, dad would be leaning against the hall railing in his boxers, sometimes barely awake. She would remember thinking how big and strong he was, and brave for getting up so early to go to work. She said this was a morning ritual until yours truly was born. She has taken that memory through life and she now knows how important it is to take care of the family even if it means you having to get up early in the morning. She finished by saying, "What may be mundane to you, is a great feat in someone else's eyes!"

The story rings true to me, I get up at 3 AM for work and I sometimes pass Courtney and Emma in the hallway as they carry their pillow and blankets into my room to sleep the rest of the night with mommy. They say they are proud of me for getting up for work so early, but they wish I was a little quieter so they will not wake up.

My brother Steve told me dad gave him advice one night before going out as a teenager. Dad told him to take two dimes with him. When Steve asked why, dad said just in case he had car trouble or just needed to call home. Steve told me to remember back then we had only phone booths, and sometimes they ate our money. Well two dime became two quarters with inflation. And now a day's everyone and their mothers have cell phones, but Steve still puts two quarters in his pocket every time he leaves his house just to remind him of dad. (God Bless You Steve, My Bro)

As much as times change, the more they stay the same. I always say to Courtney and Emma when at a friend's house, if you need to call just do it. I don't know if they know what a phone booth is but they do know all of the avenues home to mommy and daddy.

The most touching stories came from my brother Jimmy who showed me two sides of dad I never knew. Everyone use to pile into my dad's car and go to grand mom's house for dinner on Sunday nights. Jimmy said he did not know why they drove because grand mom's house was only about one and a half blocks away. About 7 or 8PM they would pile back into the car for the journey home. They pulled out of grand mom's driveway. Went about 50 yards, to the corner, made a right. Go 200 yards, make a left. 50 yards and make a left onto their street. One night dad slowed down to about 5 to 10 MPH and he opened the driver door and started to use his foot, pretending he was pushing the car up the road. He said something to the effect that he better get some gas in the morning. Jimmy said they all went nuts.

Then Jimmy turned my world upside down. Either in the fall of 1963 or the spring of 1964, dad was over grand moms as he did so often. He was driving home between 7:30 and 8PM, he accidentally struck a young girl with his car. The girl was wearing a dark-colored school uniform as she dashed out from behind an ice cream truck. Jimmy says he can still picture the sadness in dad's eyes when he got home that night.

The neighbors who shared the steps with us on our street, the father was a detective for the Philadelphia police department. About two nights after the accident, his wife came to our front door. As she walked in, my brother overheard her tell my mom that the little girl had passed away. He remembered seeing dad sitting down on the steps he was so upset. Jimmy thinks dad never got over her death.

I had to pick myself up off the steps at home when I was reading it. I was on my way down stairs to show Kim the stories from everyone. The way I remember dad from my young life, were directly from the effects of the accident some 14 or 15 years earlier. What I saw was a frail father. Now that I read this it explains everything to me. I may have been young, but I knew something was wrong. When I read Jimmy's story, I felt dad's sadness. I finally had a connection with him; unfortunately it was over something so tragic. But I felt him like I was there with him. Then I thought about him being with me when everything happened to Nathaniel. At this moment some 35 to 36 years later there is a bond, maybe through a drastic, life-altering event, but it is a bond. I know you a little clearer now, dad, the two tragedies in our lives have drawn a line to connect the two of us. It is unfortunate how it all turned out for you. I am sorry I did not get to know you better, in better times. You have guided me without me knowing it. Nathaniel's life has altered my life along with my family, now I have to turn this tragedy into something inspirational and I still need your guidance and your fatherly love to help me continue to understand. You were there all along and I didn't see it. Now my eyes and my mind are open to the future life I lead, not follow, but lead. Stay by my side and help me.

Speaking of people who step it up year after year, the people at the Arc of Frederick, MD. Kim registered Nathaniel's name at the Arc and when Thanksgiving came around we received a phone call and they told us we are going to get a turkey dinner with all of the trimmings. So on the Monday before Thanksgiving, three boxes of food were dropped off with a 17-pound turkey. Then two weeks later the Arc called again and asked how many brothers and sisters Nathaniel had, what ages are they and what sizes do they wear. A couple days before Christmas, four trash bags of presents showed up at the house for the girls and Nathaniel to open Christmas morning. Again, it is the little things that make this world a little more enjoyable.

After the cold winter season and the temperatures start to rise, Nathaniel heads back to school. This is one of my sheer pleasures in life to witness. Terry, Nathaniel's nurse, comes to work at 9:00 AM and starts to get Nathaniel ready for school. The whole time she reminds him he is heading to school on a big yellow bus. You can tell he is excited. Terry always tells him things in an excited tone of voice and he response to it. By 11:20 AM, they are outside waiting for his school bus. When his bus arrives, Nathaniel can hear the engine and the bright yellow color catches his eye. He gets so excited, he stiffens and shakes and sometimes lets out a squeal. He does not do this every day, but there is some level of positive emotion from him. The bus driver and her assistant bring down the wheelchair lift all the while we are saying goodbye and telling him to have a great day at school. When wheeled up to his spot on the bus and strapped in, mom and dad (if I am home that day) are up in the bus saying more goodbye's to Nathaniel. Terry goes to school with him and helps with all of his therapies and transportation.

Getting Nathaniel to school is no big deal, but getting signed up for school is a huge deal. The amount of paperwork and the meeting of the minds that has to be done before Nathaniel can go to school is astronomical. Everything feels like it has to be done in triplicate and done over just to be sure. A meeting must be set with the nursing agency, pediatric doctor, state coordinator, teachers and mom and dad to make sure we are all on the same page. I do not know how Kim handles all of the paperwork and I do not know how the state of Maryland and his school keep it straight. Every semester it seems the same paperwork is sent to be filled out. Paperwork is about 40% of Kim's waking hours. School, medical assistance, state of Maryland information, there is a never ending process of fill this out and make copies of this and that, get the originals of this or that and then make copies of the originals and then send them to this other person next in the paper trail so they can make copies then send the copies back to us for our files. Then the next semester, do it all over again. There has to be easier way. I know our society can survive with less paperwork, and I know why the mounds of paperwork are kept in place. Because the state or local even federal government want to weed out the serious people who need to file for themselves or a loved one. If they need the assistance, they will finish all paperwork handed to them. The governments will hope the people who are trying to get one over on them, will not spend time to fill out all of the necessary documents. There has to be an easier way. We did not ask for all of this work. After Nathaniel is registered for the first time, only updates or changes to therapies or prescriptions should be documented. Not to fill out the same paperwork originally handed to us over and over again. And God forbid if you mistakenly put something wrong or forget to put something down you put down before, they know exactly where the mistake was made and we are questioned on the truth, with and sometimes it will cause a delay in medical coverage or denial of the same medications Nathaniel has been getting for years. They are discouraging families, like ours, or individuals with the true disabilities trying to continue to function on their own. A system needs to be set up where it will be easier to control our already hectic lives. We would rather spend time with our kids, rather than filling out your tedious paperwork we filled out just a month ago. Our son's disability is debilitating enough. So many of these families are lost in the system already and it needs to be corrected yesterday.

As for Nathaniel, we do every single piece of paperwork needed because he deserves every option available to him. Mommy and daddy are his voice, his advocate's in life. We do for him what he cannot do, no matter how long it takes to fill out every single tree cut down and used for Nathaniel's information. We are here for him.

Speaking about being there for Nathaniel, one day I finished work a little early so I decide to stop by his school to see how his day was going. It was a Thursday, so that means a swim in the heated pool at school. When I arrived, Nathaniel, sporting only swim trunks showing off his one pack abs, was sitting on the edge ready for a swim with his teacher. They put on a neck floatation device to keep his head above water and his teacher lets him float around the warm water. A free, peaceful moment for Nathaniel. His body weightless, and loose as a goose. The warm water really relaxes his whole body. Nathaniel loves baths at home and I love getting in the water with him, he really melts into you when you carry him around in the water. A peaceful moment in an otherwise hectic and tragic life. It is like he has not a care in the world. He would fall asleep if you left him alone long enough.

Since the fall of 2009, Bonnie Gordon has been with Nathaniel. She is a home hospital teacher for the Frederick County School System. "Mrs. Bonnie" is not just another teacher; she is an advocate for children with special needs. There are certain people in this world who have a gift of developing the minds of children. When it comes to "Mrs. Bonnie", that gift is tremendously magnified. She is on the move every day. She travels to and from each of her student's home, making the difference in their lives. Each student has a different special need and "Mrs. Bonnie", on her own, develops each curriculum to let these children shine. Thank You "Mrs. Bonnie" for all that you do, at all hours of the day to give Nathaniel a piece of your beautiful mind. We Love You.

Another moment I love to watch him closely on is when he wakes from a relaxing sleep. It takes him about 10 minutes to get focused on his surroundings. But for those 10 minutes, he is as gentle a person can be. He stretches his arms and legs, arches his back, and lets out a long grunt trying to shake off his sleep. His eyes are usually wide open like he has that deer in the headlights look. You can also tell it is hard for him to see after he first wakes up. If you speak to him gentle he starts searching for you. His innocence is overwhelming, capturing me. Nathaniel makes me feel I should jump up in his bed and cuddle with him. The cares of my world disappear when I see him this way.

My two other cares in the world are Courtney and Emma and the time with them is just as enjoyable but more hectic. The one thing in this world I never want to happen is the girls would feel neglected or burdened with Nathaniel's health. They both understand in their own ways that Nathaniel is sick and he cannot do the things his sisters can do. The wildest thing I have seen is what they know about Nathaniel. When you are around something long enough you pick up on certain things, even kids pick up on the most unusual things. When Nathaniel was born, Courtney knew Nathaniel was sick, not to what extent, of course, but she always said to others when they visited that "Thaniel" cries a lot.

As she grew up with Nathaniel and we started to have nurses around, Courtney really picked up on medical terms quickly. Then when people come over now, Courtney would spit out words like pulse oximeter machine and stethoscope at the age of 3. A short time ago, I talked to her and ask her about Nathaniel and how she feels. She told me, in a cracked voice, on the verge of tears, that she knows how sick he is and she knows what mommy and daddy are doing for Nathaniel. She does not understand what happened at birth but she told me when she grows up she wants to learn about it. Coming from a 6 year old, I think it says a lot about what she is feeling inside.

(June 6, 2005)

(Today I had to cancel my date with Courtney and Emma because Nathaniel is having a tough time breathing and Kim thinks we may have to call 911 soon if he does not get better. Emma did not mind so much, but Courtney was very mad. She cried for a long time. I felt very bad about it. I told her I would make it up to her next week but she did not want to hear it. I finally convinced her to get her friends to come over, but it took a while for her to calm down.)

Of course, as a young kid, Courtney gets mad and upset that things are cancelled and I hope she does not resent Nathaniel for these things. At least I don't think so. She is more passive and quiet about Nathaniel. She just started to go to Sibs Shop once a month to have time with other kids her age who have a brother or sister with a disability. They do some arts and crafts and some talking if they want to but they are not pressured into talking. The whole reason behind the class is to let these young kids know they are not alone with what is happening at home. Courtney does not talk a lot about Nathaniel. Maybe as she grows she will come out of her shell about him. We always tell her that if she ever wants to know something about Nathaniel just to ask. And when something is going on with Nathaniel we tell her and Emma what is happening so they don't feel not just left out but to let them be involved in their brother's life. Today, Courtney is coming out of her shell a bit by playing little league baseball (with the boys) and she is in the third grade joining her schools newspaper staff. It makes mommy and daddy feel we are doing the right things.

On the other hand, miss personality, Emma, well she is a trip. She interacts with Nathaniel just the way Kim and I hoped she would. We wanted to have three kids from the beginning even though all of the things that happened to Nathaniel. The day we brought her home and put her in Nathaniel's crib with him, she has made a tremendous impact on his life. Nathaniel's reaction to Emma was like "who is this squirmy and crying baby in my bed?" But he also took to her like a big brother. As she grows, the interaction is beautiful. As Emma would start to crawl, she would pull herself up on Nathaniel's Tumble Form chair, smack his leg, and climb up on him. At first, he would be startled but he became use to the rough stuff with his baby sister. If she would cry he would get still and listen to hear what was happening. As Emma got bigger, she started to sit with Nathaniel in his bed and watch mommy, daddy, or even the nurse change diapers, take a temperature, check Nathaniel's oxygen levels with that pulse oximeter machine. She was curious and always wanted to help. So I would let her listen with the stethoscope or put the pulse oximeter machine on his finger to get an oxygen reading. She started to say these words and knew what had to be done with each of them. When others would see this, they were amazed at what she was saying and how she knew what to do with it.

At 2 and 3 years old, Emma is a very bright girl. She is a rough tomboy right now, especially with daddy. She likes to beat up on me, all in fun of course, but she can really hold her own. But no matter what is going on, she never forgets her Nathaniel. She will walk in on him frequently during the day to say hi or to jump up in bed with him to read a book or two or to turn on his radio. She is what we were looking for in the way of the interaction with Nathaniel. Don't get me wrong, Courtney does also but her interaction is different. She is very quiet with him. None the less, Nathaniel knows both of his sisters in his own way. As the girls grow up, I hope they realize how special Nathaniel is and how they both play a part in his life.

Going through each summer here in Frederick, MD one thing is a constant, the fireworks at the Frederick Keys games. Singe A minor league team for the Baltimore Orioles. Throughout every season, about 20 nights or so, they have fireworks with running the bases for the kids. We generally do not go for the whole game so we call the ballpark to see what inning the game is in then we pack up and go up around the seventh or eighth inning to watch the fireworks. We decided to take our video camera one night to record Nathaniel's reaction to the fireworks. What happened this night made my heart proud. The game was over quickly and it was not dark enough to set off the fireworks show. So they decide to let the kids run the bases before the fireworks this night. So for the first time we decide to let the girls run the bases and we cannot forget the man himself, Nathaniel. But we could not figure out how to get him down to the field. So we asked one of the employees directing the kids down the steps to the field how can we get him down there with his wheelchair. We were told to take him outside of the stadium and go down to the driveway in the right field corner and someone will unlock the gate for us to get in. This is where the line forms to go on down the right field foul line. We had to wait a while for someone to show up and let us in. We were last in line this night. Just as well, I knew the kids would run faster than us around the bases. Now picture this, the game was a sell out with about 6,500 fans, all of them were still there for the fireworks. So as we approach first base, I realize this will be in front of everyone. All of the moms and dads were cheering for their kids and we wanted to be just as vocal. When it was our turn to run we told the girls to run and wait for us at home plate. One of the girls who worked there told us she would wait with the girls at home. Then it was Nathaniel's turn. With mommy recording, we started out towards second base with a very bumpy ride so I slowed a bit so Nathaniel can enjoy this without being shaken up too much. Kim turned to finish taping the girls crossing home plate and Nathaniel and I are the only ones left. What I heard next was so unbelievable; I start noticing the crowd of 6,500 starting to cheer for Nathaniel. As we moved around second base, the crowd was getting louder and louder. I started to cry. Nathaniel had the biggest smile on his face you could have fallen in if you stepped in front of us. I kept telling him "everyone is cheering for you, big boy!" As we reached third base I finally looked up at the crowd and everyone was starting to stand up and cheer louder for Nathaniel. The team mascot Keyote gave Nathaniel a tap on the shoulder as we passed by as he was cheering him on. As we reached home plate the crowd gave Nathaniel his loudest cheer just as if he hit a game winning inside the park home run. Nathaniel was so excited along with his sisters, mommy, and daddy. The ovation said a couple of things to me. One was "way to go Nathaniel, don't let anyone tell you CAN'T!" And it also told Kim and I "way to go mom and dad you are doing a good job!". As we walked past the fans along the first base line, I heard some of the fans yelling "way to go, buddy!", "all-star boy!" and "Keep it up, boy!" It was like he really hit that home run. This is one of our moments in life we walk as a family together and people looked at us and were saying "There is a good family, God Bless them!" Yeah, God bless us.

It's the fall of 2005 and we are told by the owner of the house we are living in he is going to put the house up for sale but he has to move back in for two years so he would not have to pay some taxes when he sells it. Kim and I were talking about finding a smaller house with less of a rent payment anyway. We are really struggling to stay afloat. The owner told us to let him know when we find a place. We finally find a two level townhouse on the other side of town that we can move in on January 1, 2006. This sucks also because it is Christmas time. I am trying to pack a house and decorate for Christmas at the same time. I do not want to mess up Christmas time for the kids. The good news is we will be saving money moving into a smaller place and hopefully it will alleviate some of our financial headaches. We were allowed to move some of our belongings early into our new digs. As I start to do this, I realize that we are going to have to get rid of a lot of our stuff. In all I ended up making eight trips to Goodwill and six trips to the city dump in our minivan. In the course of this move and cleaning up, I find some things of Nathaniel's that put us back in time. In some good places and some bad places. The portable bassinet we tried to get him asleep in when he first came home, the body cast he wore when he had his hip surgery. We thought we wanted to keep them but now we feel we must move on. Some of his baby clothes, I gave them to Goodwill. Maybe another child could find comfort and warmth where Nathaniel struggled to find it. We also had some equipment that he has outgrown, even an extra hospital bed. I took all of this stuff to Nathaniel's school to donate it to a local family. The hospital bed went right away to a little Mexican girl in his class. I was proud it all went to use and not just sat around not being used.

(January 2, 2006)

(I don't write as often as I use to, but today I felt like there was a turning point in our lives. The problem is I do not know if it is for the better. We just moved to save money. Our bills are starting to escalate higher. I hope spending less in rent offsets the regular bills a little easier. We also have given up so much in this move, but we must move on. P.S.—Let us not get hurt! The reason I write this is to ward off any injuries. The last two moves I got hurt or had surgery after our move. Stay safe.)

We are trying to get settled into our new house and about two weeks in, Nathaniel is having a couple of bad seizures and his oxygen level has been dropping very low. So we have to call 911. Welcome to the neighborhood! As the ambulance and paramedics arrive, our new neighbors are all out checking on us. This is how we met some of them for the first time. We explained to them about Nathaniel and this could happen time to time. Of course, as Nathaniel gets out into the cold air he will be doing better by the time he gets to the hospital and he will be all smiles at his nurses in the emergency room. The nurses come running in to visit him and he will bat his eyes at them. They love it. Kim and I say he just wants to visit his women. If Kim goes into the emergency room with a flare up of Crohn's, all of the nurse see our last name on the board and they come running in but are disappointed it is not Nathaniel. Kim says she wishes she would get the same attention Nathaniel gets when he goes to the emergency room.

Two weeks later, I end up in the emergency room. Kim and I do not get to go out with each other too often, so we try to have one night out each week. By ourselves, unfortunately. Kim's is bingo night and mine is ice hockey. Well, as my family would say, "What the hell has he done now?" I was always breaking a bone somewhere on my body. Well, this was no different. No, let me rephrase that, this one takes the cake. I ended up breaking my ankle in three spots. Oh yeah, I dislocated it also. Ugly! All I kept thinking over and over was Kim and the kids and how I am going to be a burden on them. Again! With this injury, my work is going to suffer, Kim is going to be exhausted, and it is never ending for us. We cannot catch a break. (Break is not a good word to use right now.) We need a break to help us not hinder us of our efforts. I am so stupid. I should not have been playing ice hockey. I was overweight trying to get back into hockey playing shape.

The emotions I had at this time were disturbing to me. I felt like I let my family down, and especially Nathaniel. I have to be there for him 24/7. I could not say I am sorry enough to Kim and all she kept telling me was "Shit happens!" It just happens more frequently too us. Well, it sucks. From now on, it is playing cards or board games with Courtney and Emma. Kim says I am only allowed to play golf again when I get back on my feet. I think that will be a while; I really did a number on my ankle this time. Let's just get on my feet first.

(February 3, 2006)

(I am sitting here on my couch (where I have been since January 26th) and I am doped up on pain killers and I have no idea what I am writing. The one think I do know is "I suck!" What the hell, I am so frustrated with myself that I cannot see straight. Or maybe it is the drugs. I just had surgery two days ago and I have more hardware in my body. My ankle is killing me. It feels like it weighs 50 pounds. Kim brought out Nathaniel to sit with me today, I apologized to him over and over, and I started crying. And all he did was smile at me like "it's OK dad, I am here for you!" No matter how bad I was feeling, Nathaniel made me feel better.)

When I read my entry from above to put it in this book, I had to read it a couple of times because I really was drugged up at the time and I had to figure out what the hell I meant or what I was trying to say. Meanwhile, when I was down and out on the couch we finally got some good news. Nathaniel had something exciting coming to him and the whole family. He is having a wish granted by the Make a Wish Foundation. We applied with them in the fall of 2005 and two of their case workers came out to meet with us as a family and talk to us about Nathaniel, it would be like an interview. Courtney and Emma included. They want to hear from us. What happened? What's going on now and what is life like here at home. After our meeting, our report would be given to a panel and a decision would be made in about a month. Well, a month goes by and we get another visit from the girls at Make a Wish. Nathaniel's wish was granted, and we are going to see Disney World in Orlando, FL. We are so excited. Finally something good for the Breen family. First, we have to give them Nathaniel's background and information on his health, prescriptions, nursing help, etc., etc. Here we go again, more paperwork. But this time it is for a better cause, so we do not mind it all. And you know what; all of this is well needed. We have not had a vacation in six years. Courtney was only a year old the last vacation we took and she does not remember any of it. We also have to decide when we should go to Disney. Orlando gets hot and humid at certain times of the year, so Kim says we can go in October. Not too hot, not to cold. Hopefully just right. So Make a Wish will come back a week or two before we leave to give us our itinerary. I, myself, have never been to Disney so I am just as excited as the kids.

Back to everyday life for now, my work has not suffered too bad, but I am constantly have been catching up ever since I broke my ankle. I had only been working at my new job for two months when I broke my ankle and my insurance had not kicked in yet. The owner of the company tried to move up my insurance to cover my break and surgery, but we were unable to get it covered in time, at least for the emergency room visit and the surgery. The day I went to my surgery, I had to pay a down payment to start the surgery. To this day, we are still trying to pay it off and the emergency room visit and its two years later. And some of the simplest things turn into great hardships. We do not have good credit since Nathaniel was born, as a matter of fact, our debt has goon through the roof. Now a day, Kim and I laugh at the amounts of money wanted by the state of Maryland and insurance companies. I am glad we do not own a house or property; we would have lost everything by now. That is what really sucks about this damn country. Families like ours have a child or spouse gets sick or in an accident, insurance companies only cover what they deem necessary, the families struggle mightily and when push turns into a shove, creditors could seize their house or property, garnish accounts as payment due on such bills. You Creditors all suck! There should be a law added that when someone checks your credit score it should show when families have a disabled "immediate" family member so they can check into the reason why their credit is the way it is because of the astronomical hospital bills which can't be paid in a timely manner are added to our scores, we should be evaluated on a case by case basis. None of these families asked for all of this to happen. Do not even get me started on Nathaniel's equipment prices, which are outrageous. Remember back in the 1980's when some of the prices of things came out that our government was charging for some items. Like $800 for a toilet seat and, $550 for a hammer. Those are cheap compared to some of the equipment Nathaniel has at home. With all of Nathaniel's pricy items, I have to start rehabilitation on my ankle and they want me to come two times a week at $30 or $40 a visit, depending on what equipment I use. We cannot afford it. I will have to do all of my rehabilitation myself. Our $30 to $40 must go a long way in our house. It seems we have to do things ourselves these days.

The following summer was kind of a flop. Too hot to do things outside with Nathaniel, so it was somewhat uneventful. Maybe that is a good thing. But I am of the mindset we must make ourselves relevant. You know what's relevant; it is count down time for Disney World. Make a Wish called to come out to go over our itinerary and it finally hit me. We are really going on vacation for the first time in six years. And my thoughts turn to "how are we going to do this trip?" Well Make a Wish had everything thought out down to the minute getting from point A to point B. I start to think of all of the stuff we have to do before we go, while we are there and on the way back. I cannot wait to get home already. I sound like a father who is a little up tight. I said to myself, "Relax Chris, and remember to step back." as I did on Halloween. Now I feel just as excited as the kids are.

The day we are leaving, the van picking us up is at our old house. I hope this is not a sign of things to come for the week. We get to the airport and everyone knows what that is like. Well triple that with Nathaniel's equipment. We are allowed on the plane first and they wrap up Nathaniel's wheelchair to go under the plane. Over his seat on the plane, there is an oxygen tank if needed for him. The girls are so excited to fly. We arrive in Orlando and we are to meet with two of the volunteers from Give Kids the World Village. They greet us as if we were family. They call the van service to pick us up and take us back to the van rental office to drop off the gentleman who picked us up. We then make our way to the village. From this moment on until we leave, we are in the world of fantasy and we are to leave the real world at the door. For the next week, we had not a worry in this world. Nathaniel and the girls were treated like the prince and princesses they really are.

The Give Kids the World Village was founded some 25 years ago by a gentleman named Henri Landwirth, a gentleman from Belgium who lived and survived concentration camps of Nazi Germany. A survivor of the Holocaust, he came to America and founded a dream with the help of American businesses who donated everything for the special kids like Nathaniel and their families. I had no idea this place excited. I just thought we would be right in Disney or just outside the Magic Kingdom. What we did experience was beyond our belief. From the moment we arrived, we were swept away from our everyday lives and we were treated to the time of our lives.

We had our own villa to stay in. A huge two-bedroom flat. Some of our day-to-day occurrences were the same. All of Nathaniel's every day equipment and his necessary needs were already there waiting for us. And our nursing company in Frederick was the same in Orlando, so we had the same schedule of nurses we had at home and the agency only had to fax our information on file to Orlando so we did not have to do the dreaded paperwork. Our first night, the kids and I checked out the village while Kim went to an orientation for new guest. The village had something going on every day and every night for the kids and parents. The coolest thing was that everyone there was sent by one organization or another so these kids would have the time of their lives. Yes, these kids are sick or disabled, but it all seemed to disappear when we were all together. Our hectic lives are their hectic lives. We have all walked the walk in our separate lives but we all ended up in the same spot. We know what the families at the village are going through.

When together, I felt we were one whole family. It was like a family reunion and you were meeting some of your relatives for the first time. You knew about them, but to finally meet them was refreshing. I did not feel sad for anyone the whole week. The smiles told it all. When mommy rejoined us, she showed us all of the things we can do at the village, but the real concern from the girls and daddy was when we could go to the Magic Kingdom. Yeah, I was caught up in the moment, leave me alone. Of course, on our first full day, Sunday, we hit the Magic Kingdom. Television does it no justice. The vibrant colors and the immaculate conditions were spellbinding. Now here was the thing I really had to get use too, and at first, I felt uncomfortable doing it. We saw our first set of life size characters. So Kim said lets go and get their autographs. We bought the girls autograph books, which I highly recommend, it keeps the kids busy and they do not want to buy everything they see. Nathaniel had a poster with his name on it welcoming him to Give Kids the World Village and Disney World. So Kim decided to use it to get Nathaniel autographs. He also wore pins of the Village and Disney. When the park employees see these pins, they automatically hold the line for Nathaniel and the girls and the characters would spend a little time with the kids and sign their books and take a few pictures or video. I felt a little uneasy doing this at first. We would walk up past 30 or 40 people (mostly kids) and butt in line and hold it up. The amazing thing, I only heard (aloud) one woman say something all week. She said, "What makes them so special?" I thought to myself, Nathaniel does, this is his moment. And he loved it. He loved it so much; he sat in his wheelchair for 5 or 6 hours a day and did not complain once. At home, he would complain going across town to the doctor's office. I guess he would rather have Disney over the doctors, but who wouldn't?

Monday was the most special day in dad's heart. We visited the Animal Kingdom. The most riveting moment of my trip and yes, my life, happened here. We arrived when the park opened and I was told to go see The Lion King Show. So we went to the very first show of the day. About 500 people packed into the show, and of course, we were ushered to the front of the line with Nathaniel leading the way. We were given front row seats with a spot for his wheelchair. The seats were arranged in a circle with a middle staging area. Courtney just wanted to go on the rides and thought this was just wasting time. Suddenly the lights went low and the fog came out of the ground all around us and the most elaborate show of colors and costumes appeared before our eyes. Characters were coming at us from every direction. Some on stilts, some on trampolines, just so much going on at once. It was awesome, we were all blown away.

Towards the end of the show, a woman dressed and painted like a zebra walked up to me and said, "Can he walk?", pointing to Nathaniel. I told her no. So she said, "OK!" and wheeled him away. I thought to myself "What just happened?" She took Courtney and Emma, too. They are going to be in the show along with about five other kids. The zebra girl was showing the kids what they needed to do to be in the show and you could tell she was asking if Nathaniel could shake the maracas. It then looked like Emma went on to tell the zebra girl Nathaniel's medical history. She then finished explaining to the girls what to do for the next part of the show and off they went, dancing around the stage with the entire cast of Lion King. Of course, I was videotaping all of this and was so excited for the kids. It was another one of those step back moments but this time the kids were enjoying something I never got to enjoy because this was my first trip to Disney also. Courtney quickly forgot about going on all of the rides and skip these stupid shows and Emma was marching around like she owned the joint. But when Nathaniel came back around from the far side of the stage, we all could have fallen into his mouth. He had the biggest smile on his face. I could hardly video tape it; I was crying and felt so happy for him. I was so proud of my kids. But that is Disney, you leave your troubles at the door, as Simba tells your son, he is the chosen one. That is what it is all about. I cannot say it enough.

After it was over, I asked Courtney what she thought about the show. She could not say enough either. Day three we went to Sea World and

Universal Studios the next day with trips back to the Magic Kingdom to see the nighttime parade of lights and fireworks. When back at the village we could swim, mini golf, take in a movie or play in the game room. We never stopped. Everything was taken care of for us. Breakfast and dinners were inclusive, all of our park passes were free, and we were even given spending cash for the week. Make a Wish Foundation really gave Nathaniel a dream vacation.

Reflecting back to our day trip over at Universal Studios, we made our way through the park and I noticed a couple of families who had children in wheelchairs and started to wonder if they were from Give Kids the World Village. By this time in our trip to Orlando, I was wanting to talk to these families to get there initiation stories into the fraternity of disabilities, but so far this day I didn't have a chance to catch up to any of them.

So we went on with our trip through the park taking pictures, the girls got their faces painted, Nathaniel met Shrek and I was just taking my step back and enjoying my family in the moment. We decide to go see the Barney show. Now Courtney and even Emma were over Barney at their ages but Nathaniel will always have a spot for this big purple thing and his friends singing and dancing in front of him. So we get in line for the upcoming show, and of course, we were ushered to the front of the line for the handicapped section and the rest of the lines were filling up quickly. There still was about 15 to 20 minutes to go before the show, when one of the families I saw walking around the park came up in line right beside us.

The child in the wheelchair was a boy and he had a brother and sister close in age to Courtney and Emma. Kim and the other mother started talking as if they had known each other for years. With the unfortunate similarities between our families, there was a lot to talk about. This family was visiting from Sweden, but not on vacation at Disney. They were there for the medical appointments they had in the state of Florida. I started to listen in on their conversation when I found out that the Swedish government paid for the family to come over to America for medical appointments with doctors here that are experts in the field of their child's disability. I was so intrigued by what she said. Then she blew my mind when she said she had been to Moscow to see a doctor who then referred them to the doctors in Florida and their government paid for all of the expenses. "WHAT?" And "WHEN CAN WE MOVE THERE?" She told us they pay a little more per year for their healthcare coverage than we do but they do not pay for doctor visits, blood work, x-rays or tests. They just pay a yearly fee. This fee covers everything, and as you can see, I mean everything. The mother said she researched doctors and treatments for her son and found a specialist in Moscow, so off they went, check in hand. Then they were referred to a practice in Florida. So off they went, check in hand. They then thought they could visit Disney while in Florida. Check in hand for this also. The mother put it this way; we may pay a little more yearly, but whatever is needed for any member of the family to get them well, they get it. I was floored.

I said to Kim it was like a blank check for a healthy life. We spent a little more time talking in line and after the show, our families were asked to hang around for a private visit with Barney and friends. Our sons, from different parts of the world, were enjoying a moment or two together, which they will never realize, but they shared a joy of friends and family. I told Kim we are moving to Sweden. I wish we had something like that in the United States, but I know that will be way too much to ask. And I know it would fall on deaf ears no matter how far up the political ladder we went. We need a person to step up, go against the grain, and make a real change in our world.

Back at the village, Nathaniel was given a mirrored star. We wrote his name on it and the year. Before dinner on Wednesday night, we are to take the star to the castle of dreams and deliver it to the fairy treasure chest and make a wish. We were told by the fairy that the next day we could come back and look for Nathaniel's star on the ceiling of the castle. So after dinner on Thursday night we go back to the castle and sure enough his star is shining bright on the ceiling, right near the middle of the castle. This is another one of those step back and check out our world moments. Along with Nathaniel's star, there are thousands upon thousands of other stars covering this massive main room and side rooms of this castle. The names of all of the children who spent a piece of their precious lives here at Give Kids the World. A moment in time for every star. A moment well spent by a family together. This moment will never be realized by Nathaniel in this lifetime, but my family will cherish these moments for him forever.

This week was filled with some of the happiest memories of my family to date that I will carry with me for the rest of my life. It also restored some of my faith in people of this world. The thing most impressive about

Give Kids the World, it was run mostly by volunteers and the amount of the volunteers throughout the year is astronomical. People who give up their own time for children with disabilities are very special individuals. And it rubbed off on Courtney and me. After Christmas, Kim and I saw an advertisement on a lawn sign near our house for little league baseball sign-ups. Courtney wanted to sign up and try out. She thought that girls' softball would be too hard yet because the ball is too big still, and it would be hard to throw. She made the East Frederick machine pitch team (with all boys) and she played very well. Halfway through the season we were asked to volunteer as a player and as a parent, for the Frederick Challenger Baseball League. The league was formed for the kids with disabilities so that for about two hours they were on the same playing field as the other kids. And I have to tell you, watching these kids and watching Courtney help these kids, it warmed my heart. Courtney was asked to stand with one of the players and help them field the ball. She seemed thrilled just to be there but she really jumped at the opportunity to get involved. She was very vocal with these kids, telling them to "get ready" and "I am here to help." She would help position her baseball buddy and as the better and stronger hitters would come up to bat she stood in front of her buddy so they would not get hurt if the ball was hit to them. As a dad, I was asked just to cheer on these players and I was more than happy, too. Seeing the smiles was remarkable. The craziness of life was gone for the time being. Like there was a dome around the baseball field and nothing could penetrate it. From the warm-ups to the final out, lives were made happier one person at a time. I received the paperwork for Nathaniel to play and now he can have an opportunity to be involved in an activity with other kids his age. The Challenger League was formed some 27 years earlier was the perfect activity for Nathaniel. For the first time he will be on a level playing field with kids his age. The league was formed so kids with all disabilities could play our nations pastime at their own pace. Nathaniel becomes a Brown Bear and he gets his first baseball uniform as his first baseball practice is fast approaching. The practice coincides with picture day and the first meeting with his Brown Bear teammates who come from all walks of the disabled life. When I would tell Nathaniel that it's time for baseball, he gets so excited. His head turns back and forth and his legs and arms stiffen straight like he is going to jump out of bed and get running.

We arrive at the field on a beautiful sunny Thursday night. We meet all who are involved with the league and the Brown Bears along with three other teams. They start off with a team picture. The players on his team have Cerebral Palsy, Down's Syndrome, Epilepsy and Autism. But it all seems to go away and takes a back seat to baseball at this time. And these kids know the game very well. A few years earlier, the Brown Bears went to the Challenger Little League World Series and then with an invite, went and played at the White House.

After the team picture we had a chance for some individual shots and we picked Nathaniel's pictures to be printed out as baseball cards. I never had that growing up. Then it was time to hit the field. Every kid gets a chance to bat once an inning and whoever is the last hitter gets to hit a homerun. Once in a while the team in the field will record an out or the batter will smoke a line drive to the outfield fence when batting. With all of this going on it makes my heart swell with pride and joy for these kids for these moments should be cherished by all who witness it. They try so hard and give everything they can every time out. All troubles go away and the field is their world. At the end of the season all of the teams play at Harry Grove Stadium where the Orioles single A farm team, the Frederick Keys, play. The excitement goes through the roof this day as they can play on the same field as their heroes play. Courtney and Emma put on their uniforms and are the baseball buddies for some of these kids. But that won't last too long, after helping a bit, they noticed some of the Keys players coming out for their warm ups. They would go over and say hi to the players. Kim yells down to me to look out in the outfield. Courtney and Emma are out in the outfield having a catch with the Keys players. I was jealous! Kim yells to me "focus!"

Moments of joy and no limitations. Moments of togetherness. Moments that will last forever. For me at least, I don't know if Nathaniel will remember but we will do the same thing next year and I will make it just as exciting for him. What a blessed season with blessed players and their families.

(June 28, 2007)

(I have not written in a while but I feel I have too now. I am writing a book but I felt I should write in my old journal because it is like an old friend to me. The time is coming to say goodbye to mom. My brother Steve called me and mom took a turn for the worse. I have to go and see her. Say a prayer.)

I could not keep writing in my journal, I was getting way too emotional. So I waited until now. It is the end of October, close to November 1, 2007. All Saint's Day. I am going to write shortly here about a saintly person I knew. I called her mom. She passed away on July 2, 2007. 80 years young. Back on her 70th birthday, I wrote her a letter to thank her for being my mom. I called her the "professor" and that I was so honored to take her class in life. She had a spill at home and broke a bone near her pelvis. As she was rehabbing in the hospital, she had a stroke. It was caught early enough by the nurse in the hospital that after that she still had her wits about her. She was there mentally, but physically she was damaged. She spoke with a slur and she could not use her right side. At her age, the time I thought would be short. But she was a strong willed woman all her life who believed in the cure for all ailments was vitamins. When she took her turn for the worse, I had already planned the weekend up in Philadelphia. Aunt Pat was always being shuttled back and forth by my brothers and sisters and I could tell she needed a break. So I planned for me to come up and I would pick her up and go see mom at the nursing home then I would surprise her by taking her to the Phillies game that night. Both of us were seeing a game in the new ballpark for the first time. Patsy and I eat, drink and sleep baseball. It was our first live game together since the 1983 World Series game three at the old Veterans Stadium. We enjoyed ourselves tremendously, even though they lost (what else is new) but this break was well deserved. The following day, I visited mom by myself. She woke up briefly to acknowledge I was there. I told her I loved her and it was OK to go and see dad. The backbone of our family, the most dedicated, unselfish person I have ever met was about to go on her long awaited journey beyond this life. Heaven received a MVP (Most Valuable Person). Her soul was blessed here on earth; I can only imagine what it is like in heaven for her. She must be doing back flips. God rest your soul Mom, you deserve it.

Even though mom passed away, many great memories came flooding back to me. One, when times were at its hardest for me about Nathaniel, mom tried to make me realize that God is with us and we can get through this no matter how long it may take, and things might not turn out the way I planned it. She always pounded that into my head. I said a couple of choice words without thinking a couple of times, but she never tried to stop pounding it into me. I thank you that for mom. Things are clearer. Not all of them, but I now know why you never gave up telling me about God.

A lot of good vibes (even with mom passing) really go back to our trip to Disney. One thing after another was going our way, and it makes Kim and I feel good. Our family was functioning at our highest level possible. Kids are happy and are learning to deal along with mom and dad. Never ask the question "what could go wrong?" because the dominoes start falling. My work asked me to take a drastic pay cut. Business sucked and I was being paid a draw against my commissions. Plus, the place I was working had a turnover ratio of salespeople greater than the amount of customers coming through the doors. I got our friend Brenda (you remember her, the crazy lady who said she would watch my children when I had no clue who she was. Yeah, her.) a job where I worked also. Along with the seasoned retail sales veterans I worked with, Brenda fit right in and made huge advances in such a short time, and was asked to work for $300.00 a week as a single mom with two kids. You're welcome Brenda; she will never let me live this one down.

The seriousness of a pay cut forced me to look again for another job. My never ending task in life. Listen, I never finished college and I barely got by in high school, so my work skills are limited. I never had made more than $32,000 dollars a year in my life. This last place I was working at, I found out I was making as much as the receptionist. I give my all everywhere I go. It sucks so much that I have such a hard time keeping a job and I have been finding a couple of jobs I really love but ever since Nathaniel's birth it's been like I have been going through a revolving door consistently. I have always made a great impression wherever I work and have made friends with every one including my boss. But business is business and when I miss work, my work suffers, and I am looking for a new job. I cannot tell you how many friendships I have made just from my work experiences.

My most recent search for a job was a struggle. I was about to bite the bullet and work retail again. This means long, hard days on a commission-based salary. We need the income, but the hours suck on my family. I am all about family, of course, but when I spend twelve 12 hours on my sales leads and I am closing on average 15% of my customers. This sucks, because it means I will put twelve 12 hours in for work and that will leave twelve 12 hours for my family and I would like to get seven 7 hours of sleep, if possible, so that leaves five 5 hours for my wife and kids. When you have a disabled child and two active young girls, five 5 hours will not cut it. So one of the jobs I accepted on a Friday, I rejected on that

Sunday. On Monday, I went back to my job hunting. I put out a couple of resumes, even filled out an application at a fast food restaurant as a cashier. I am a proud person, no job will embarrass me, hell at this point, and I will mop the floors with a toothbrush if it paid enough.

When I started to do some research about families with sons or daughters with disabilities, a redundant statement kept coming up on the father's side of things; it was constantly getting harder to keep their jobs or as the years went on, the amount of jobs they were trying to keep were adding up. When I said, "I would mop the floors with a toothbrush," I was not kidding at all. It sometimes comes down to desperation. Man, I have gone on interviews where the people would look at me and say, "Why are you here?" "You are way over qualified for what we are offering," or in the same breath, "You have no qualifications at all for the position being offered."

I can tell they are starting to look at me like, "What is wrong with this guy?" "There must be something going on with him." I have gone as far to tell them straight up, "My home life is hard and I am looking for a job as simple as possible because when my wife or son get sick and need something more than a day of rest, I have to stay home and take care of things. So when I am fired or let go or have to leave my job, it does not sting as bad. Forget about having a career. My next career move should be as a nurse so when I graduate, I can get a job with my son's nursing agency, stay at home, take care of Nathaniel, and get paid for it. This will never happen because it is a little thing called a conflict of interest or nepotism.

I would like to start my own business at home. OK, with what money? Even those cheesy ads you see that say, "Start your own business and live debt free for the rest of your life!" "Just send us such and such amount of money for your informational DVD to see what we have to offer and then if you are ready to live beyond your means, send us such and such amount of money to get your start-up kit. Do not forget shipping and handling." Again, with what money? And where is my toothbrush? I figure if I tell these people at interview time what my dilemma is, maybe they would understand what I am going through and see my honesty and integrity and I would get a chance at the job I am applying. But it will always backfire because they see how much work I may be missing if these things happen, they will not hire me in the first place. And I am even talking about any job. My job searches are for jobs I can get in and out at my set times. Maybe some overtime, but no more 12 hour days, trying to convince someone to buy a product that is way over priced to begin with and then hear someone above me question my ethical standards (which are high) on why I am not selling their products.

Not one of these people want to hear my sob story, they want and need results. Some jobs I totally believed that "this is the job for me and my family" and I make the most of my opportunity. But one thing will lead to another and we split ways, usually with a pat on the back or a phone call from someone ripping me about how I became very undependable and I really cost the company money. When you are wanted and needed it will make you or anyone a stronger person, but when you get that pat on the back, or "sorry it is not working out," or "I cannot do this anymore," it is belittling. I start to question why I keep doing this. Then I start to look in the classified ads and see the same ads repeatedly, I put the paper down, look at my family, and think how inadequate I am to them, and there is no lower feeling. Desperation sets in. I have had moments of anger. I have yelled at my wife and kids for no reason. I would give my shirt off my back or an arm or leg to have February 14, 2001 over again so I could scream and yell harder, maybe even kidnap a doctor to deliver my son earlier. All of this for my little guy who lies in a hospital bed in our den/dining room of our townhouse we rent because we cannot get a mortgage because of our lousy credit.

Now what? This cannot be happening. Kim is starting to feel like she has something wrong in her stomach again. She must go to the emergency room and get it checked out and she heads out the door to the emergency room on this warm Saturday afternoon in September. I tell the girls, "Let's get moving on the cleaning of our house for mommy." Top to bottom. Clean, dust, vacuum and all of our clothes away. The girls are on board with me, even Nathaniel pitched in. He broke through his diaper and wet his bed. So I have to change his bed and give him a bath. We knock it out within four hours. Kim will be so surprised when she gets home from the hospital of how well in a blink things change around our house. Unfortunately, Kim will be the hospital until the following Thursday, another one of her five-day journeys into the hospital. The Crohn's really plays havoc on her body at times and it happens more times than not. This time, just like last, she has an obstruction in the same spot, due to scar tissue from a previous resection surgery and inflammation due to a flare up. Stress also plays a big part of Kim's problem. We unfortunately have plenty of stress around here.

What Kim needs is a doctor of her own, not a team of rotating emergency room doctors in the hospital. The Veterans Administration has gotten her a doctor to see on a regular basis but he keeps cancelling appointments with her. Or they do not see or understand the sense of urgency of her Crohn's Disease. One doctor said to her one time that he was not going to prescribe some pain medication to her because her pain could not be that bad. A week later, after Kim had a colonoscopy, that doctor walks into her room and says "I guess you were not kidding about the pain." The colonoscopy showed her intestines were lined with white-headed ulcers. Again, here is the example of another doctor who does not listen to Kimberly when she knows when something is wrong. Most of these doctors and nurses know Kim by now, please listen. So while Kim is in the hospital, I have to shake things upside down. First I have to ask the state of Maryland for more nursing hours for help with Nathaniel. This is like pulling a tooth some times, and by the time Kim comes home we will finally get the OK. I have to arrange help with getting the girls off to two different schools in the morning and I usually cannot get the same people every day, so I set up a rotating schedule. And I can only work a certain amount of hours because my help can only help for so long. So here I go again with screwing up work again. It was OK for this time but it will wear thin the next time and the next time.

Well the next time was only two weeks later, and then two weeks after that. Four hospital stays in eight weeks. Kim said her surgeon is running out of options so the next flare up will result in surgery. And it has done just that this next time. Kim has had her third resection done in 14 years. My life at home is so out of whack, I do not know if I am coming or going. Kim's mom came up from Myrtle Beach, SC to help me out. She has been a godsend. I do not know what I would do without her. My father-in-law is at home fending for himself. I owe him for letting me borrow his wife for a spell. On the other hand, he is a Redskins fan, so he can fend for himself.

So there are the lives of the Breen family for the past six years and nine months. What do you think? Crazy? You bet! And you can bet there are other families out there that have it worse than us, that is for sure. We are a fraternity of families that have been truly wronged. We fight to exist every single day. We fight for the loved ones who are damaged. We fight for the right to be sane and have a normal family life, which we may never see. But we will never find that out, if we do not stop trying. We must push forward and try not to look back. It is hard to stay focused when you think back on why all of this happened and it is the reason we are the way we are. I sometimes think what our lives would be like if none of this shit ever happened. We can only hope for Nathaniel to be comfortable, well and happy, and that is a tough thing to control at times. We will never stop trying, for sure.

CHAPTER VI

My Son

My son, Nathaniel Ryan, whose life has not turned out the way he wanted it to be, whose life was altered at birth, who unknowingly touches the lives around him, whose unconditional love can never be matched, is my hero. My son has been through more trauma than anything I have been through in my life, yet he smiles consistently. He will never speak to me like a toddler to a young daddy, or a growing boy to a dad, or a strong-headed teenager to a strong-willed dad, or a college-bound young man to a proud father or even man to man. But you know what, as he battles for his life every day, he babbles to me or yells out, I know what he is saying and feeling. There is a connection that I cannot explain and he has the deepest love you will ever find. It is what I call . . . let me see . . . Unconditional.

I am humbled by Nathaniel. There is a line in the show "The Sopranos" in which Tony's mother says, "OOOOHHHH poor you!" I started out thinking this way. I would say, "Why is this happening to me?", "Why Kim?", "Why us?" Then I would feel sorry for us and myself. The way I had my life planned out is gone. Then I started to really think, "Hey, it is not me, it is Nathaniel!" His normal life is gone. Then I felt selfish, even guilty. I found myself constantly telling Nathaniel, "I am sorry!" My guilt ran deep in my soul and it made my sorrow deeper and deeper. In addition, of course, you start to think of all of the things you could have done to prevent this mishap and I start to blame myself for his injuries. If only I stepped up and spoke aloud, our whole family would not be in this mess. Kim and I have tried to right the ship repeatedly, but as soon as we get to where we like to be, which is comfortable, something comes along and knocks us back down. All through the difficulties, Nathaniel just lies back and takes it all in. This is all he can do. My poor son, he did nothing to deserve all of this. He will never crawl or walk, sit up on his own or even talk. He yells out and babbles at times and sometimes it seems he is trying to mimic what he hears from you. If you catch him when he is on his game, it looks like would talk forever. It is as if it is on the tip of his tongue and he is about to spit it out, but he is trapped in his body. I really feel for him, I know he is in there. When we talk, it seems he knows what is going on. We get some reaction out of him and it is always paid off with a smile. The kind of smile that makes your day. Sometimes he gives you his half smile, which is when one corner of his mouth goes up. It is the cutest thing to see. Then you have the "fall in the mouth" smile where he is ear-to-ear beaming. This smile last the longest as if he gets lockjaw or something. The unfortunate thing about the smiles, after they are gone sometimes it is like Nathaniel is gone, too. He spaces out and when you do the same thing that triggered the last smile he does not give you any reaction, like it never happened. This happens all too often, unfortunately. One minute he is there, the next, nothing. His brain injury is severe and I always hope and pray it does not get any worse, like when he has seizures, do they do more damage to his brain? Or will that next seizure be the one that kills him.

We work so hard to keep Nathaniel comfortable. All of our energy is spent on the wellness of Nathaniel. He has about nine different medications he takes, most on a regular basis, some when needed. As he grows, the medications have to be adjusted. We try to wean some of the medications off and add new ones some times to try to balance him out. Right now, we are at a good mix. The seizures are under control, for now, so Nathaniel is comfortable (knock on wood). Nathaniel has a ton of equipment that is a tight fit in our tiny house. We use to have a Tumble Form chair that he could sit up in on the floor with the girls, he had a Gate Trainer which that he could get in and it would help him use his arms and legs in a crawling position, but he could never move in it, too complicated for him, you know, no motor skills, he can't do it. The simplest of activities for a growing toddler. Seeing him set up in the Gate Trainer upset me. I wanted to just get him started moving his arms and legs, but there was no effort or reaction.

He was also given a stander. This would help to strengthen his torso and also to work on keeping his head up. To Nathaniel, his head is just a 10-pound weight, but at times when he is on his game he really works hard to keep his head up, it bobs up and down a lot but it seems to work when he wants it too. Nathaniel can only stay in his Stander for a short amount of time. The scoliosis affects his ability to stay straight in the stander. Nurse Terry says he will put on his "angry eyes" when he is ready to get out of that stander. The most frustrating thing is by the time he gets the OK for the equipment, then is fitted for them, then has to get an approval for them, then finally receives the equipment. There is a lot of time that is wasted, and that Nathaniel is constantly growing, he barely fits in them when it arrives or he can only use them for a short amount of time. And his time is very, very important. I do not how much time he has and I do not want to waste a second of it.

After having that Tumble Form chair for a long time, Nathaniel was cleared to get an adjustable chair with all of the bells and whistles he needed. If you never heard a person gush over a chair as much as I am about too, it will be a first. From the very first moment we put Nathaniel in that chair, it was a saving grace. That chair was abused so much by Emma climbing all over Nathaniel and the chair and Courtney and her friends running circle around it and rocking back and forth in it and being turned upside down so all of the kids would slide down it. It took a beating, but for Nathaniel it was peaceful. It was the best seat in the house. He listened to his sisters grow up around him down at their level and him and daddy would take in a hockey game next to the television as he watched the shadows of the players going up and down the ice. Or Nathaniel would just get himself relaxed enough he would take a peaceful nap in a crazy world. That chair was as close to him as his family. The best part of Nathaniel's new chair is the height adjustment. Instead of just being at floor level, his chair can go up to table height so he can sit at the dinner table for family dinners or when his sisters are playing or doing arts and crafts at the table. The unfortunate thing is the chair is so bulky; it is hard to fit it at our dining room area because of how small the area is now. Kept in this area also is his stander and his wheelchair. Most of the time, as in mom and dad and the girls, can hardly fit for dinner in the dining area. Coming with Nathaniel's new chair, it has a plastic tabletop you can slide into the chair so he can do some of his therapies while sitting up in it.

All of the equipment will help better my son's life somehow. If in his lifetime he can do only one of these things himself, our lives would be fulfilled. I know it is impossible, but we can only hope and pray, can't we? The one thing I think that is the most rewarding with Nathaniel is when he yells out or babbles. There is a boy in there who wants to be heard. He has great timing also. Kim and I could be talking to the girls or each other and all of the sudden we would hear Nathaniel yell out from the next room. Nurse Terry gets the biggest kick out of it. It is as if he is chiming in on our conversation. We always go running into his room and bring him into the conversation and he just keeps on going almost as if he is mimicking us. He also has that gentle voice time where he is just full of love. If we are having a bad day, you we can walk up to Nathaniel and he would put you us at ease. When he gives you us the gentle voice, it is as if he is telling us, "What's the matter dad?" "Everything is going to be OK!" It really makes me forget what I was worried or upset about. At times, I slide him over in his bed so I can climb up in bed with him and totally forget about the world outside of Nathaniel.

Other moments that are remarkable to me is when Nathaniel hears Courtney, Emma, and their friends around him. Especially when Emma makes time for him. She will climb up with him, with no prompting from mommy and daddy, and she will get him involved with whatever she is into at that very moment. At first, he feels her climbing up and over him and he starts looking for her. As soon as she speaks, he knows it is her and gives a big smile and is almost like, "OK, what are we going to do today?" Emma will usually turn on his radio or read a book to him. Nathaniel will be paying attention to her intently. At 4 years old, Emma really knows her stuff. She will play doctor with him sometimes and she will use all of his equipment correctly, while Nathaniel does not mind being a guinea pig; he loves the attention from his sister.

With all of Nathaniel's disabilities, he does have some type of recognition of who we are, and he sometimes does things to make us think he is just stuck in there somewhere. Ever since he was born and he had all of the tubes coming out of him, all I wanted to do is let him hear and feel mommy or me. How scared and confused do you think he was when he started to come around after his birth. He did not feel his mother or heard daddy and Courtney in the background. All he heard was that damn monitor beeping in the N.I.C.U., a sound that I will never forget and still haunts me to this day even if I hear it up close and in person or on television. He was being poked and prodded and was hardly moved at all. He could not even cry out because of the damn tube down his throat. He was alone without his family for periods of time while in the hospital. You have to know these kids feel this on some level. I believe no matter what state of consciousness; a newborn has it in them a trigger to give them that familiarity of at least mommy. Kim was heartbroken when we were told we could not hold him. What if Nathaniel passed away without mommy holding him? I thought of this driving home from the hospital with Courtney one night. I then thought he would have never felt that loving touch from mommy. I believe every woman has this power in her. But imagine a child passing without that touch. They would have never felt a gift of life, the warmth of the skin and soul of their mother. I was afraid of this happening to Nathaniel and Kim. Of course, for me also, but especially Kim.

As you have read, Nathaniel is a strong boy. The shit he has gone through has been remarkable. I must say unfortunately by mistake. Why is he still here with us? What is the reason for why this is happening? And yet, he comes through every time. I guess these are the questions to be answered later on, not in this lifetime. He has courage that he does not even know about. He has no say in the decisions mommy and daddy make for him, but he goes along with us nonetheless. It is almost as if he can take everything you throw at him. If he could talk he would say, "I'm still here! What is next?" When we were faced with the scoliosis problem, I looked at him and said, "no surgery. No, I cannot do this to him." Kim said the same thing. We did not make up our minds because of the arrogance of a doctor, which who still deserves a good ass kicking for how he treated my wife. All we had to do is look at Nathaniel. Look, if he had more going on for him in this world, I mean crawling, walking, doing things on his own, and then of course we would go on with the surgery. I would never forgive myself if we lost him due to selfishness. He has been through enough pain. His whole life has been one big pain.

Yet he moves on and just smiles at us, now with some teeth missing. Just like any other 6-year-old he is beginning to lose his baby teeth and he has not let us get one of them yet. He had swallowed the first three he lost so far. Kim wants one of his baby teeth so bad that she has made me check his diapers when he goes poop in them. Yes, ladies and gentleman, I check the poop. No luck so far, but finally, nurse Terry noticed a loose tooth up top. So she springs into action. She was not letting this one get away. With accurate precision she snagged the loose tooth and reported it to his mother. Mission accomplished. Thank God. I was tired of digging around after the fact. Nathaniel looks so adorable with his missing teeth. And he knows it, too. The tooth is now a part of his life memorabilia.

Nathaniel's life memorabilia is different than Courtney and Emma's. When Courtney was born, Kim bought me a book for daddy's to write in about their daughters growing up. I guess many of the questions can be answered for a son also. Its questions are about life's accomplishments and how I felt when my child accomplished these moments. I looked through the book recently, I applied Nathaniel to some of these questions and a lot of them I could not answer and I never will be able too. As some of the questions are so simple, they are all things we take for granted. It made me sad to think what we take for granted in life, Nathaniel will never accomplish. You try not to think about it. Kim likes to focus on what he can do. They are all very small feats but they are Nathaniel's feats and we always congratulate him on them. He deserves the same amount of praise Courtney and Emma get.

As Nathaniel grew, we started to notice that a regular car seat was not cutting it anymore. So he was fitted for a Kid-cart (wheelchair). Then we realized that the mini-van was getting smaller with Nathaniel's bigger equipment. So we started looking into buying a wheelchair accessible van. Of course, with our credit and the prices of large vans through the roof we cannot afford to buy one. But we found out that the state of Maryland has a program where they would let us be eligible for a very low interest loan through the state. There are regular stipulations, but not so drastic. Not too far from us there is a mobility company who sells used vans with wheelchair lifts or vans that can be converted into wheelchair accessible. Getting this van makes our lives so much easier. All we have to do is keep Nathaniel in his wheelchair and the girls fit comfortable on the bench seat in the back. Lugging Nathaniel around is a chore, for sure, but this has made our lives a little less stressful. Nathaniel is now on his second Kid-cart and for the rest of his life; this is how we will get him around.

I wish I could climb in him and undo all of the problems caused at birth. Unlock the boy who I know is in there. I sometimes wonder how close is Nathaniel. How close was he to being a normal, healthy, 7 year-old? How close is he to being able to speak to us? I catch myself looking at kids his age and I imagine Nathaniel running, jumping, pulling on his sister's hair, covered in dirt head to toe. It saddens me to think of this every time. His disabilities totally outweigh his possibilities by far. What does the future hold for Nathaniel? We know with the scoliosis getting worse, his body will change and it will not be for the better. We could see problems with his respiratory soon, and I do believe we may have already begun some changes already. We asked for a vest known as an "airway clearance system" for Nathaniel. It is a vest he wears and it is hooked up to a machine that will force pulses of air throughout the vest rapidly and will keep his chest a lot clearer of mucus. This vest has been a tremendous help. We have notice a huge difference on how clear it keeps his chest. But of course, it still will be a never-ending battle of health. If we do not stay two steps ahead of any cold or fever, it could turn out much worse real quick. Other problems caused by the scoliosis would put pressure on some vital organs. I do wonder when we talk about this, do other people look at us and think why they don't do something about it. Believe me, I do not hear it, but I see the expressions and it still bothers me. I'd rather be trying to decide what ice hockey skates fit Nathaniel best or show him how to hit a pitching wedge at the golf range. Instead I feel uncomfortable talking about why or why not to do thing to save the life of my son.

My best friend in this world is Tom Aughey, who has two sons, Thomas and Tyler. Thomas, who shares a birthday with yours truly, plays ice hockey for the Jr. Flyers and other club teams in the West Chester, PA area. Well I finally got an opportunity to catch one of little Tommy's games on a weekend I was back home for a wedding. And I was so thrilled to see him play, but when the kids hit the ice, I thought only of Nathaniel. This should be him out there with Tommy Jr. learning the game Tommy Sr. and I played growing up. Well, I played ice hockey all of my life, I never saw Tommy on a pair of skates, but we played some awesome hockey (dec-hockey) in a league in Aston, PA for years. But when I saw Tommy Jr. and his fellow teammates, I felt that hole in my life with Nathaniel. Here is something I did all of my life (until I broke my ankle) and I always thought I could pass my passion on to a son, and I could live vicariously through his love of the game. I started to cry. It was so hard not to imagine Nathaniel out there on the ice. I tried to hide my emotions. I do not know if Tommy saw me or not, but I was hurting emotionally. I had to leave early to get ready for the wedding. And I went back to Tommy and Elaine's house and cried in the bathroom just thinking of my boy at home in a hospital bed.

If there is one thing I could pass on to Tommy and Tommy Jr. is to cherish every damn moment you can. Live that dream through your son Tommy, he is going places, I know it. By the way, Tyler, who is younger, wants to be a goalie just like his Uncle Chris. Tommy, hope if you do not mind, I would like to live vicariously through Tyler, maybe he could stop those center ice shots. Do not laugh.

Nathaniel and I did have a somewhat of a hockey moment together. In the spring of 2005, I was playing in an adult ice hockey league here in Frederick, we played late at night most of the time so Kim and the girls could never come out and see me play. Kim used to go to all of my games, but when the kids came along I went to the games by myself. This one night a surprise came to me. We had a late game, I think it was about 10:00 PM, the referees were late getting to our game, so both teams were skating around shooting pucks waiting for the refs to show up. That is when I looked up, and to my surprise; I saw my family coming in the rink from the far entrance. Kim, Courtney, Emma and guess who, my boy, with the biggest damn smile on his face. Courtney and Nathaniel had off from school the next day so Kim thought she would surprise me. Well, she sure did. I went right over, opened the rink door, and said, "Give me Nathaniel!" He was all bundled up with coats and blankets; you could barely find him under everything. I was so glad the refs were late. I took Nathaniel for a skate of our lifetime. I was pushing him around the whole rink as fast as we could go. His mouth was wide open with laughter. I swing by my team's bench and introduce him to everyone. My teammates jumped off the bench, welcomed Nathaniel, and patted him on the arm and chest. I was so excited for him. He was stiff as a board with excitement. We wheeled around the rink a couple more times just to soak it all in. The refs showed up and we had to play hockey. I bent down and whispered to Nathaniel "I just had the time of my life!" and I would never forget his smile when we are doing something I wish we could do every day together. This moment in time was exactly that, a moment. Well about 8 minutes. The best 8 minutes I would ever feel with the joy of my son.

After the game was over, my teammates and myself would always have a beer together in the locker room. (Gatorade for me. No, really!) The guys start to ask me about Nathaniel. They had no idea I had a child with a disability. They said I did not act like it. I said, "How should I act?" I tell them we go through a lot of shit as a family. I told them hockey was my break from everyday life. Every time I leave the rink, I always go over the game in my head, this night I had no idea that I even played a game. All I thought of was my skate with Nathaniel. Over and over, I would think of his huge smile. This was a chance for him to experience something I do in life. A chance for him to experience something other than a hospital bed. I have no idea if he knows what he did or will ever remember one second of anything in his life, but he made my enjoyment of ice-skating that much better. The night I broke my ankle, I knew I was not going to play hockey again or maybe even skate again. The only thing I thought of when I was being helped off the ice that night was that short skate I had with Nathaniel and his smile. That big smile.

After healing my ankle, I would repeatedly find myself thinking of the ice skate Nathaniel and I had together. I would say to myself, "I wish I could skate with him again," but I promised myself and Kim no more hockey or skating. But why is it that I threw out all of my hockey equipment except my skates. Maybe someday. Right? Well my mind started racing and I thought, "Maybe we could go for a skate." Not for long, just a quick one to see that huge smile on his face. I do not know if he remembers our last skate, but as I say all of the time, I will always introduce things to Nathaniel over and over. It is what I enjoy, and if he remembers, even better.

I started to look up public skating times when I noticed an ad on the website for sign-ups for the Frederick Fury kid's teams and I thought maybe I could get Nathaniel to skate with a team in his age group. I sent an e-mail (with the computer I am renting) to the Fury about Nathaniel and how maybe he could skate a couple of minutes with one of the teams. I received an e-mail back saying the Fury would be delighted to accommodate our request and would contact us with a date that would suit both of us. It was a Saturday afternoon practice near the end of their winter season. We were invited out a little early to go over what Nathaniel can do and meet his teammates and their families. One person missing this day was Kim. She was in the hospital unfortunately and I will elaborate on that story later.

We met with Sylvanne, the director of the Fury hockey teams. When he approached, he introduced himself right away to Nathaniel. I played with Sylvanne briefly before I broke my ankle, so we kind of knew each other. I introduced him to Courtney, Emma, Nathaniel's nurse Rashanda, and her daughter. Sylvanne thought maybe the first thing we should do is go to the locker room and meet Nathaniel's teammates for today. They were all kids Nathaniel's age getting suited up for practice. Today they wore their game jerseys. When everybody was ready, Sylvanne introduced everyone to Nathaniel. Each kid came up and said hi and gave him a nudge or touched his arm. Nathaniel was so excited. Sylvanne said they could not go on the ice until they were all in their uniforms. That is when Sylvanne pulled out a Fury jersey with N. BREEN sown on the back and the letter C on the front shoulder. The Captain's C. Nathaniel was the honorary captain for today's practice. I was so touched by this gesture. My senior year in high school, I was the captain of the varsity hockey team. Nathaniel and I have another great connection I will always treasure. They were making this very special for the both of us.

It is now time to hit the ice. We were going to rink #2 and as we went through the door to the rink, we met all of the players' families. They gave Nathaniel a standing ovation. This was great. I had my skates on and ready to go too. The Zamboni left the ice and it was time to skate. To me it was like riding a bike, right on the ice nice and smooth. Nathaniel's mouth was wide open yelling like, "I do remember this, dad!" We skated around with his team. After a warm-up skate, we all got together for a team photo with Nathaniel right in the middle. Courtney, Emma and Nathaniel's nurse went around to the player's bench. They shot some video and took many pictures along with some of the parents of the players. Then we skated some drills. I pushed Nathaniel into the net to let him feel the netting and the cold post. I picked up a frozen puck with some snow on it and let Nathaniel feel it. He may have been over stimulated but he loved every minute of it. We skated for about an half an hour and we had our fun, and it was getting cold for Nathaniel, so we told Sylvanne we were done, but his teammates were not. The team gathered around him and presented Nathaniel with a bag of Fury memorabilia and they gave him a hockey stick signed by each player on his team. We were overwhelmed by what everyone had done for Nathaniel. We went off to another standing ovation and all of the parents came over to say hi and tell Nathaniel of the great job he did on the ice. The Fury went above and beyond anything I could have ever asked for Nathaniel. Thanks to all of you. And guess what, I did not break an ankle. All of the video and pictures will help mommy feel like she was there. My feet hurt a little but it was worth it. Courtney and Emma are now saying you that I can skate again so I have to take them skating as soon as possible. I should ask Kim first.

Nathaniel and I enjoy our walks even better. The weather has to be just right for us to take a venture out. When we do, Nathaniel lights up. We take the same route most of the time so maybe it will have some familiarity to him. If it is just Nathaniel and I, you know, the manly men in this family, we walk with real confidence like real men do. I love to point out everything to him, even the sounds that surround him. The motorcycles are the best. Especially the loud ones. The more I talk it up about the motorcycles or the way I react when it gets loud, Nathaniel stiffens with excitement. I love his reaction, like he is saying to me, "Dad, can we get one of those?"

We see some of the same neighbors every walk. Some of them come up to us and always say hi. This interaction for Nathaniel is therapeutic. Some of them have asked, "What happened?" or "what is wrong with Nathaniel?" some just give a friendly hello. When I tell people what happened to Nathaniel, I can see the sadness in their eyes. They have all said sorry to me but a few have said sorry directly to Nathaniel. I always feel that is the best compliment of sorrow. When it is said to Nathaniel, Yeah, he may not understand, but it makes daddy feel good when they say it directly to Nathaniel. It means they understand his plight. Yeah, it does affect the whole family, but they went directly to the source.

I look at our walks as therapy for the both of us. I get to show my son our little corner of the world around him and it shows Nathaniel a world he really does not know but if a motorcycle flying by with a loud roar, or we hear a bird chirping in the trees above us, or even a friendly hello from a neighbor will make Nathaniel smile or yell out or even babble, daddy is proud. It makes me feel I am doing my job as a father. All of these things are so minuscule in the big picture of life, but for my son's life, they are the highlights which that he may never remember. I will. I do not know if he ever will. If he survives another long cold winter, and the weather warms up, will Nathaniel remember the motorcycles or the birds from last year? This is what disturbs me and hurts my heart. On the other hand, I love to teach him every day. Even though it may be the same things over and over again. I will never stop. It does encourage me to try harder. I try to make everything spectacular for him. The way I say things, the way I let him feel things, these walks are important to the both of us.

These walks around the neighborhood or at the mall or wherever are not only good for the both of us, I believe we touch the lives of others. Every person we come in contact with walks away thinking or saying something to a significant other about Nathaniel or our family. At least I hope we do. I always say I want everyone to know Nathaniel because I think what if. A professional athlete to a neuro surgeon. You never know what he could have been. By making a glove save in the seventh game of the Stanley Cup Finals or saving a life of a child or adult with a brain tumor. Doing the things like these, you really touch the lives of others. How Nathaniel does it right now, people walk away may be feeling sorry for him. That is still touching the lives of others. I hope that person walks away thinking of how lucky he or she is with their family, health wise. Maybe they go home and give their loved ones a hug just to give thanks or they sit around the dinner table and mention they saw us out and about and they discuss how that family gets by each day. Now let us think of the flip side. I wonder if there is anyone out there who may have encountered us and thought or said, "What the hell are they doing outside or walking around the mall with that kid?" Come on, I know you are out there. Who thought this? There is always one somewhere. With all of the negativity in our world, how could you not? I know it was said somewhere along the line. Shit, someone in Kim's family suggested to her we should have let Nathaniel die after birth. Yes, die. This is what I call selfishness. This is the reason he is with us, not with that family. There is a poem we have displayed in our house called "Heaven's Very Special Child." Within the poem, it reads the angels are telling God "let's be careful where we send this child. They want his life to be content." Well, we are those people and proud of it. It took a while to figure things out, but we are managing.

The most powerful and touching moment in my life came while I was out with Nathaniel and my family. I hope I explain this story well so you can feel the touching moment as I did when it happened with Nathaniel.

(April 14, 2003)

(I was wrong tonight. Not all people think we are different. An older gentleman showed me not to judge to fast and I now know we are making a difference. I am proud of myself for being strong in a difficult time.)

In April of 2003, we decided to go out for some dinner as a family. We even packed up Mom and Patsy so we can enjoy each other's company. We had to take two vans and we went over to Cracker Barrel. We put two tables together to sit comfortably. The restaurant was busy, as usual. Kim put Nathaniel's wheelchair at one end of the long table, slightly out in the aisle. We had to move him a couple of times so the servers can get around easier. The wheelchair is just plain bulky. And Nathaniel never really like sitting in his wheelchair for long. You could see how uncomfortable it always was for him. So just before our food arrived, I decided to pick him up out of his chair and hold him. He was being fed through his feeding tube at the time, so maneuvering him was even more of a task than the normal routine. As our food arrived, I finally get Nathaniel situated on my lap. I ask Kim for help cutting my dinner for I only had one hand available but at least Nathaniel was finally comfortable. As Kim was preparing my meal, I noticed an older gentleman watching my family and me. He looks away every time I look over at him. I then notice him commenting to his wife and using his hands to point out to his wife we moved two tables together so we could all sit as a family and that Nathaniel's wheelchair was sticking out in the aisle. His wife had her back to us so she would try to sneak a peek occasionally but she did not try too hard. As dinner went on, I would catch this gentleman watching Nathaniel and me more frequently. I started to feel a little uncomfortable, but by this day I was learning to pay no mind to what others were doing or saying, I was just enjoying my family. Suddenly, Kim pointed out Nathaniel was starting to have a seizure. So we immediately shut off his food. The seizure was strong enough to cause Nathaniel to choke and vomit. So Kim and I spring into action. Since Nathaniel's stomach surgery he cannot throw up out of his mouth, so we have to vent his feeding tube into a plastic bottle. Calmly, and I reiterate, calmly, Kim grabs a bottle out his bag, I sit Nathaniel up as straight as possible. He is coughing and retching, but his tube is open and relieving his belly. Customers of course notice us scurrying to help him; even some of them ask if they could help us or call 911 for us. We calmly, and I reiterate, calmly, handle everything with ease. Nathaniel finally settles down, and so do mommy and daddy. I check out the older gentleman to see if he is looking our way. Both he and his wife are starring right at us. The conversation, which I could not hear, seemed to be a little upsetting to them. I felt we were making them upset and uncomfortable, as a matter of fact, I felt we were making everyone feel this way. To compound the matters worse, Nathaniel has another seizure, not as bad as the first one, but we were more prepared for the second one.

We as a family hardly react to something unusual happening. Again, the older gentleman was watching our every move. By this time, I just wanted to finish eating and get Nathaniel home. We were still trying to figure out our way of life and how we could function normally. Kim and I switch a couple of times holding Nathaniel. When our dinner was over, we start packing up and I was putting Nathaniel's coat on when suddenly someone tapped me on my shoulder. I turn to find the older gentleman standing right behind me. It only took a second for him to say what he had to say, but within that one second so many thoughts went through my mind on what this guy is going to say to me. I thought we were going to have a confrontation. And then I heard him say the kindest words anyone has ever said to me. He said, "If there were more fathers in this world like you, our world would be a better place!" It took a second to register what he said. When I realized what was said I started to tear up and then he said, "I just wanted to shake your hand and wish you and your family luck!" He turned to Nathaniel patted his shoulder, walked back to his wife, helped her with her coat and then they were gone. Kim walked over to me and asked, "What the hell did he say to you?" I was so choked up I could not even speak. Mom always said never judge a book by its cover. I do not anymore. That gentleman made an impression on my life that will always be with me. Those words meant so much to me and I told Nathaniel what the man said and that we are touching the lives around us. Nathaniel just gives me that half smile like he is saying to me, "I know dad, and we did good."

That half smile means the world to me; it is Nathaniel's sign of Unconditional Love. A love that has no boundaries with us. Think about it, Nathaniel will go through life without sin. All he has is love. He knows no other way. Kim and I will never have to correct him or send him to a timeout. He is as close to being a true angel among us. Now to say all of this is nice, but to think of the reason why we can say these things, it is due to human error. I'd rather be raising Nathaniel like his sisters. I know he would be tormenting the girls to no end. So you can imagine the rollercoaster ride of emotions. We move on day after day while Nathaniel just lays there in his hospital bed.

We do believe he is in that body somewhere. To what extent? I do not know, and we may never know. But some times, he reacts as if he understands what we are talking to him about. He gives you a very sly look every once and a while. When it looks like he is focusing in on you, you truly feel his love as if he, at whatever age, wants to learn from you, or like he cannot wait to hear what you have to say next. I go to him some times with thoughts and the troubles I have with day-to-day activities and no matter how I feel, Nathaniel will put a different spin on things. He will try to focus in on me and give me his ear to bend. He gets quiet and listens sometimes. I know I can depend on Nathaniel to listen because of two things, I believe it is therapeutic for both of us and we never want to leave him out of our conversations or family activities. What I try to get out of this is a piece of mind. I love talking to him. Nathaniel may not see that well, but his hearing is exceptional, so it is important to keep him involved.

He wants us to keep up the talking and keep up the noise; it is his involvement with the family. He shows he cares. I do not know if any other people see it, but we do. If we are out somewhere and he hears a child cry nearby, he gets very quiet and listens and his expressions will change. And maybe someday with all of the redundancy of what we do day after day for him, it could possible click in his mind, if only for a moment, I would love to have my son. This day may never come but I can wish all I want.

Other wishes and hopes I have are to quicken (not just for Nathaniel, but for all disabled children and their families) the process for every available resource out there for these children. As I touched on earlier, the paperwork and the red tape we all have to go through is astronomical and I am fed up with it. I feel the families of these kids should not be questioned ten 10 times on the same issue. We do not have time for this. Nathaniel does not have time for this. His life is too precious to waste on paperwork; then again, his is just looked upon as a number or a statistic. He is not trying to get one over on you, and like I said before, you know who you are. Nathaniel needs these resources now not later. Every moment counts.

I know I have a limited amount of time with Nathaniel and you can say we are fortunate to have him with us. We were told a couple of times that Nathaniel would not make it to his third birthday. I do not know if that was said because of his health issues or that the family, mostly mommy and daddy, cannot deal with the situation and they give up. Well Kim and I never ever gave up. As bleak as times got, we always rallied each other. But there is something that Nathaniel has that keeps him chugging along time after time. Does he know it? Probable not, but he has this unknowing will power to survive. He fights back and gets better. Everyone's body reacts differently to the situations handed to us. I have seen bigger people crumble, mainly myself. If I get the flu, I am the biggest baby. Nathaniel, whose immune system is weak due to his injuries, gets better every time. It may take a little longer but he gets better. Kim and I have sat with Nathaniel many times in a hospital room or behind an emergency room curtain wondering if this is the time he will not recover from whatever is affecting him. The most astonishing thing with Nathaniel, while all of this swirls around him, he smiles. Stomach surgery, hip surgery, 103 degree fever, it does not matter. The one thing I think of is that we show him nothing but care and love. He knows no other way.

From day one when we brought Nathaniel home, we have devoted our lives to three things. One, keeping Nathaniel comfortable and as healthy as possible. Two, raise Courtney and later on, Emma, like a normal everyday family. And three, for Kim and me not to lose focus on our love for each other and our family. Yeah, we struggled. We struggled mightily, but we keep our focus and or tired minds open and today I am proud to say Courtney and Emma are two growing beautiful girls and Nathaniel is still with us, and OK health wise I must say (knock on wood), eight years after the third birthday deadline that some doctors say he would not get to see. Nathaniel had as much to do with it as his family did. He is strong, and still I do not know how.

We can speculate forever on what could have been with Nathaniel's life. I would hope he tried his best in everything he did. School, sports, friends, work, girls. You always hope that your kids would have an easier time in their lives than yours. Kim and I have struggled with our lives since Nathaniel was born. He struggles just to stay alive. So far, no matter what he is up against or how sick he gets, Nathaniel comes through with flying colors and he surprises us every time. This all comes very natural to us; we just go about or lives' without batting an eye. Even the girls do not get upset with what sometimes happens around our house. We could be trying to get Nathaniel out of a illness and if we are not succeeding we can call 911 for help and an ambulance ride to the hospital and the girls could sit there and watch cartoons, not paying any attention to the four or five paramedics running in and out of the house. Our shock value is gone. We look at it like, "been there done that." People ask us how do we handle everything with Nathaniel and we say, "just look at him." How could you not put aside your life in exchange to help and nurture a disabled child? Nathaniel has created a greater level of love in our lives than we ever expected. He has taught us to be humble and have patience beyond our means. He makes us realize how important our lives are and how much he needs us. I could be at work in one of our balls-to-the-wall moments and I start thinking of Nathaniel. I wonder what he is doing at that very moment and if he is OK. He is never, ever far from my mind. He is my life.

When I speak of Unconditional Love and Nathaniel, what I get out of it that he will never understand it or learn what it means. But he receives it from others and he gives it away unknowingly. He does not have any conditions for love; he just takes it as it comes to him. He is our most precious gift in life. Yeah, I wish things were different, but we cannot change the past, we can only try to make his future healthier and full of love. And living a life, no matter if the life is Nathaniel's, or as imperfect as daddy's, without a sin or misbehaving is an amazing feat. I know it is not me. I use to tell my mom, "Think of Nathaniel this way, if he was around when Jesus was alive and Jesus asked said, "let he who is without sin, cast the first stone!" Nathaniel could be that guy. Hey, look at that, I quoted Jesus and I did not get struck down by a bolt of lightning, he still must love me. I know he does, I just have a terrible time trying to find my way back to him. More on that later. Let us go back to the man of the hour. Or in this case, lifetime.

On December 5, 2007, Nathaniel laid sick with a fever and severe congestion that we are working on vigorously. Could this be the beginning of the end? NNNNNAAAA! Not the way he fights. His body will fight off this just the way you and I do. Longer? Yes. Again? Yes. What can we expect down the road? I do not know. His orthopedic doctor says his hip could dislocate again as he grows, the scoliosis is gradually getting worse and we could be one major seizure away from a fatal one. So many things for such a young man to deal with but he does not worry about it, he lets mommy and daddy do all the worrying and we attack it with a positive attitude. If we didn't have that positive attitude, I guarantee Nathaniel would not be here today. Nathaniel will feed off this positive energy and that is why he knows no other way but love. Unconditional Love.

I do not know his outcome in life. I have an idea, but who wants to think of that now or for a long while. I will not stop telling and teaching my son all of my ways, my memories, my intuition. I will do some of the same things next year when the weather gets nice and we go for walks or run the bases at the Keys game or stick our feet in the sand box at Baker's Park in downtown Frederick. And I hope I make a connection with Nathaniel that has some familiarity to him like "we did this before, dad." If I do not connect with him, and of course how would I know this, I must treat it as if we are doing this for the first time, this will make me excited anyway to do everything for him all over again. Just like the movie Groundhog Day. I will do it day after day for the rest of my life to show my son I love and care for him. I missed out on things fathers and sons do on a normal level, but our level is special. I never want Nathaniel to feel alone without a daddy. He listens for us with excitement. He can always hear us from the next room; he practically breaks his neck at times turning his head towards the small hallway to the living room. He wants to be so involved with everything, but being trapped in his body, not able to get up and run to his mommy and daddy and sisters does sadden me. So we go to him. We make him involved. We carry on around him and he will chime in. Kim will go to him and playfully tell him, "no yelling at momma!" She will turn him on his side and playfully spank his butt. Nathaniel will yell louder or bust into laughter, just daring mommy to do it again. Of course, mommy will go after him again and he loves it. This is the part of all the little things in Nathaniel's life that makes him special.

What else can I say? I think I told you every moment of Nathaniel's life. At least those special moments and even the hard ones. Come to think of it, every moment is a special moment. The rollercoaster Nathaniel has been on since he was born has no brakes. His life has had so many ups and downs; I do not know how he survives. When I said I was humbled by Nathaniel, I was thinking of my son going through his life with the possibility of no advancement in skills or the ability to create a better life for himself. He will always have to depend on the help of others. I see a boy who never received a chance to select his own path in life. He was robbed at birth. But, with all of this being said, Nathaniel is love.

The heart of a lion. When you introduce yourself to him, he steals your heart. He makes you realize how special all of our lives are and he gives you hope that if he can battle with injuries and so many illnesses and come back strong every time, it's like he challenges you to get off your ass, get yourself better and make something of your life. All of this from a boy who is damaged. He has no idea what he has done for the lives around him.

Nathaniel, I pledge to you two things. First, my heart. Which you have already stolen from the very beginning. My heart cries for you. You have touched my life in a way I could have never imagined. I sometimes lay my head on your chest to listen to your heartbeat. It is stronger than you think. Not just physically, but emotionally. When I hear it, I feel your love. This is my emotional therapy.

Second, I pledge my soul, which you have captivated along with mommy and your sisters. For a while, I was a lost soul (sometimes I still am lost) but you have pulled me back time and time again. I still wander about at times but I come to you for inspiration. Your life is so important to me. No matter how many times we do new things or we do the same routine, the people who you have touched will be there for you. Maybe we can learn from your love. I see it every day no matter what; you're there with a smile. It may only be a half smile, but it is all love. It is never ending. It is pure. It is truly Unconditional.

I Love You, Nathaniel. Someday, not of this world, we will talk, Father to Son, man to man. Whatever it will be, I just want to talk to hear the real you, my buddy. I Love You my Son.

CHAPTER VII

My Soul

You do realize, I rather be out front of my house with my three children playing anything, not ever thinking of writing a damn book about my son and how we are trying to survive. My son was going to be someone special just like you and me and it was all taken from him and it tears my inner being, my soul too pieces. I could live the rest of my life writing 24 hours a day about my anger and hatred, but I would be such a sour person. Pussy-footing around mistakes irks me to no end. We were so close and now we are living on the edge of our seat, day to day, watching our bills skyrocket and try to think of where our next dollar will come from.

I am tired of struggling. I am tired of watching my wife worry about things and then her Crohn's Disease acts up and she ends up in the hospital. I am tired of telling my girls we cannot do this or we cannot do that because we have no money to do any of the things their friends are doing. I have a job. I work my ass off. It is bitter sweet coming home from work every day. Bitter because it haunts me when I return home and see my only son lay in his hospital bed, helpless, not able to move on his own, not able to get up and run to daddy and say hi. Sweet because I can run to him, scope him up in my arms and bear hug him. My worries wash away. I look at my wife with her ear glued to the phone, as she stares angrily into space, probably on hold for some time waiting for an answer she does not want to hear or getting the same answer she received yesterday, which is still wrong. And it hurts to look into the girls' eyes and tell them, "We can't!" Since Nathaniel's arrival, fatherhood has been the most troubling time in my life. When I first became a father, I learned and adjusted as I went along. Courtney and I were a great connection, but unfortunately, I had no immediate connection with Nathaniel. I was torn. You know how you dig deeper in your soul to get things done or you bite the bullet and strive harder to make things work? There is that feeling you get when you reach for that extra push and have a sense of accomplishment and you say to yourself, "I DID IT!" That spot was taken out of me, held in front of me and ripped to shreds. I was as low as a father could go. I felt it was my fault. I can't even look into Nathaniel's eyes and say sorry enough times. As much as times and things change, my buddy will always be a little boy. His brain injury has caused him to be stuck in his frail body. For however long Nathaniel will live, he will pretty much be a six month-old who cannot see.

The night I found myself on the floor of the chapel at the hospital the silence was deafening. Not just here physically, but emotionally and spiritually that God abandoned us also. Every time I cried and asked why, that silence returned. God had no answers for me, there were no signs. I had distorted feelings and moments of pure rage, after I calmed down I was glad that no one was around me because there was no telling what I would have done. People would say to me God has a reason for everything. They say there is a purpose behind every move that was made. I would tell them "Bullshit!" "There is no God!" "If he was here he would not be about neglect. He would, if God was around, not let something like this happen to a newborn, innocent child!" I was enraged by what was going on. When I picked myself off the floor in the chapel that night, I know we were alone in this world and I had to gather ourselves together. Forget all of this mess. I told myself, "If they cannot look us in the eyes, you're not there."

We were talked down too; as if this kind of shit happens every day, and we know nothing about what was going on. This alone tore me apart more and more as each day past. There was anger then in a blink of an eye, I found myself being calm for Courtney and playing afternoon tea party halfway in her cardboard box. I was so confused I used to go to the bathroom and cry my eyes out and try to regroup. I did not know who to turn too. My mom told me to go and talk to a priest, but I had lost my faith in God and a priest would be the last person I would want to talk too.

My hatred ran deep, but I had to control it for my family. Juggling my emotions was an everyday practice. I was burning my candle at both ends trying to keep my job, trying to do my part at home and sleeping. Nathaniel cried just about 24/7 for the first year and a half of his life.

When we would lay him down after he fell asleep, he would wake up crying immediately and it wore so thin on us. The one thing we learned to control is the "line". The "line" was what you never want to cross. There were many a time we had to walk away and take a breather. I could have lost my mind if you I did not do it.

My focus in life changed. I now knew I had to step up further than I ever did before. I felt my love grow stronger for my family. We were a team with a disadvantage and we had to start to find ways to make things work better. Making the strides to do the right things, in my mind, were being done in spite of God or in spite of mom's always kind words. I was having to prove to them that we could do all of this without their help. We stumbled so many times (we still do), but we always try to make everything as normal as possible. The easiest of tasks turned into major headaches. If we want to go out for dinner or to visit family, we must start getting ready three to four hours before we leave. But we do not let that stop us from the attempt of normalcy. We must push forward, no matter how exhausting it may be. From 2005 to 2007, Kim and Nathaniel have missed two out of the last three Christmas Day gatherings at her aunt's house. Nathaniel always seems to get sick right at Christmas time, and he ends up in the emergency room on New Year's Eve two out of the last three years also. And then Kim's Crohn's Disease has gotten the best of her those times also. The girls and I just go and try to act like nothing is out of sync. At times when we go out and Nathaniel and or Kim are at home sick, I find myself in a zone where all I think about is them at home, or I start thinking could this be the time Nathaniel cannot get over an illness. Kim can certainly fend for herself, but Nathaniel needs that 24 hour care. Then all of the sudden Kim has needed that extra help, too. Her Crohn's really had acted up the last half of 2008 to the point where she needed another surgery to alleviate a blockage and since then is still having some trouble with pain in her tummy. I do worry about Kim just as much as Nathaniel. She really scared me this time around with the Crohn's. I have the two of them in different situations that really are life threatening. Kim's Crohn's is eating away at her belly and you they can only operate so many times to resect her bowel. And Nathaniel teeters with pneumonia every other week.

When Kim was in and out of the hospital for five times in a 10-week span, we did something we never have done before. We had our first fight. Yes, I did say first. In the middle of Kim's hospital stays, she would come home and a week later, she would be back admitted to the hospital for the same thing every other week. I felt we were not getting the proper care and attention and I started to get upset with the way things were progressing. So one night the girls, grand pop and I went to visit mommy in the hospital. I must have struck a nerve with Kim because she went off on me when I asked to see the doctor and wanted to find out what the hell is going on. Kim took it the wrong way and thought I was saying I did not believe her about what the doctors were saying. Well, she laid into me something fierce and I tried to defend myself to no avail. The fight lasted all of five minutes. The longest five minutes of my life. I absolutely hated myself to let Kim get so upset when she had been going through all of the ups and downs of the last 10 weeks. I was going through them also and it was wearing thin on me, too. Our friend Brenda was there with her fiancé Lance. Brenda said that was the first time she saw us fight or yell at each other. Kim and I told her that was our first fight ever. Brenda said we made her sick. She said; "With all of the crap you two have gone through, this is your first fight?" Yes! From the very first time I met Kim, we have had a connection like no other. Kim and I never had to work to be in love. We knew from the very first moment we were made for each other. Our souls have been blessed. Maybe those people are right when they said God has a reason for everything.

Maybe God had a hand in it when our paths crossed for the reason of Nathaniel. Maybe he knew how the two of us together would handle a child with a disability. I do not know. What I do know is that Kim and I have grown stronger from the soul on out. When we met I knew she was my soul mate. Then we go through everything with Nathaniel. I was OK with the reality of my soul until Nathaniel was born and then I felt the abandonment. I felt I was numb in my heart and soul. The one thing I did know is that I had to nurture my son. Give him the care and love he deserves and needs. As much of the raw nasty feelings I was having, I also knew my family needed me. This was a huge test of wills for Kim and me. I also believe it tested Courtney as much as she had no idea what was going on, it had to affect her somehow.

So I was being torn in 10 different directions, and how do we get past the struggles of our lives? We really don't. All of these struggles are still there. Some are gone like Nathaniel's consistent crying and some are new and growing like medical bills. But they become second nature to us when we go through them day after day. We wake up and get things done and don't stop. The one thing that has not stopped is my revolving door of employment opportunities. 14 jobs in 11 plus years. This makes me feel so inadequate at times. It is disheartening to receive a job and letting people down. It feels like every move we make, or everything that can go wrong, centers around Nathaniel. But I can never blame him for our problems. I would love you to walk in our shoes just for one day. My dreams for my son have been destroyed and I will never forgive. I have lost sleep, wages, vacations, time with my daughters and I have lost time with Kim. Her Crohn's Disease has been one flare up after another. I know the stress of Nathaniel has caused her Crohn's to be off the charts. Nathaniel and Kim deserve a better fate and I will give them everything I have to give. I honor them with my prayers and I honor them with my soul. I cannot leave anything on the table any more. My time and effort are too precious. And what can I say about Courtney and Emma, they are so brave and they do not even know it. They put up with all of this shit day after day. They have done well with everyday life so far, but will this burden them in the future? Will it affect their emotions? Will they need help to cope? They both understand Nathaniel is injured, maybe not to what extent or why all of this happened but some day they will and I hope they never forget him and all of the things they missed with Nathaniel. I want Courtney and Emma to have their own simple destiny, their own walk in life, not altered by their brother's life.

What does all of this mean? Why Nathaniel? Why our family? I tell him every New Year's we made it through another year and I hope the next one gets better. Of course, I start to cry and say I am sorry. I do this every year after the ball drops. I look at him and I am sad. He just smiles and coos at me, then he yells out and laughs, like he is telling me "I know dad, it's OK." To me it is not OK. I try to tell him I will make it better for our family this year, somehow. As I talk to Nathaniel, he tries his darnedest to focus in on me. And I look at him watching me and I always think what is the meaning of all this? What is the meaning of our lives?

I just asked the most frequently asked question in the history of mankind and do you think I know the answer? As I ponder this question, I think I have the answer. At least the meaning of my life. I have walked through life with a "just being glad I am here" attitude until I met my wife, where my focus turned to my significant other. When Courtney came along I was scared but confident with whom I was, I had the husband part down, now I had to learn to be a loving father. When Nathaniel arrived, I knew how to be a father, two years running, but now I was scared again, scared for my son's life. I was angered, I had rage against my fellow man and it took over me all the while being a loving husband and loving father. What a mix. A mix no one should feel in his or her lifetime. I was hurt emotionally, which lead to physical hurt. I put on weight I didn't need, which I still have today. I had a terrible problem trusting others, especially doctors and nurses. I could not leave my children with others right away. Kim and I would try and explain our lives to others, but no one could understand the scope of our painful lives, or of Nathaniel's pain.

Then we are trying to survive day after day. In our house, it was hour after hour. As you can imagine days started to run together and the nights were never ending. But with all of the crying from Nathaniel and mass confusion of fault and blame, we were making it work. I have no idea how, and I don't want to know how either. We started to get clearer answers about Nathaniel, mostly blunt answers, but we needed it to be said that way. They were straight answers, nothing sugar coated. Then we researched and learned to cope. Then we decided to have a third child. People looked at us as if we were crazy. We felt cheated when Nathaniel came along, we were missing a child's innocence and Courtney was missing out on a brother or a playmate. Along came Emma with enough energy to run a nuclear power plant on her own. She showed us all what was missing, the interaction of sisters and brother. It was all glorious. Yeah, as they grow, the girls will get on each other's nerves but they love each other, Nathaniel can always depend on Emma to stop by for a story or a checkup.

Have I found my spot? Maybe. I do know am a loving husband to a compassionate wife and father to three very beautiful children. My journey has been confusing but fulfilling. I work on it every day to make it stronger. I have been given a task to help a boy who has been damaged, who needed a caring father figure and he was given to me. Who knew, it was me. Nathaniel has had me wrapped around his finger from the moment I saw him with all of those tubes and IV lines sticking in him. I did not realize the damage or to what extent, but I knew from that very moment, if he made it through this I was to be the guy by his side for his life even though I was clueless on what to do or how to take care of a disabled child. Like I just said a little while back, we moved on, and we didn't even realize it. After Emma came along, I sat down and said to myself, "well, here we are, this is my family." I love it. Then I realize I have two daughters four years apart, a father's worst nightmare. Growing daughters. I do recognize our hands will be full, so I have to be prepared. Calling all dads again, we are the first role models of the opposite sex for our girls, make it work. Make them safe. Let them feel your love.

Then there is Kim. My partner in crime. The women who I have given my best and I still have so much to give. If I don't say it enough, there is not enough words for it. We do lean on each other so much but our balance is unmatched. We have been given a challenge that was truly unexpected and so heartbreaking and we are trying so hard to stay afloat. I sometimes look over at Kim and she looks so exhausted with her Crohn's Disease, and Nathaniel's life, and the normalcy of Courtney and Emma. You can feel her dig deeper and never complain once. I give Kim "I Love You!" cards or text messages with what my heart feels that day. Her 39th birthday present was the chapter I wrote about her in this book. (Guy's, jot a love note once and a while, it works so much better than diamonds.)

I learned my love note writing is very much like my dad's. After my mom passed away, I went through a box I had of mom and dad letters to each other. Most of my dad's letters were from when he was in the Army stationed in Alaska. They had a great romance also. The one thing I really took away from their letters is that I hope my love is what my dad's love was for my mom. These are my words and my love poured onto these pages. All for Kim, my beautiful wife, you have my heart.

Not too long ago something happened that affected Kim greatly and I never saw it coming. When she told me what happened, it saddened me. We were at her cousin's wedding, all was well, and it was great to be out without the kids, which is a rare moment for us, so we love to take advantage of these moments for some mommy and daddy time. The wedding was beautiful and the reception was in full swing. So Robby and his new bride Lisa were going down the list of the reception basics. First dance, cutting the cake. Then it came time for Robby to dance with his mom, and it was beautiful. But Kim had to excuse herself to the bathroom. She told me her Crohn's was acting up, so I didn't think anything of it, just a normal day for her unfortunately. Instead, Kim was thinking to herself she would never have a chance to dance with Nathaniel at his wedding. When she said this to me, I was floored. This was something I never thought of and believe me; I thought I imagined everything we will miss out on with Nathaniel. It was hard to swallow. I saw the sadness in Kim's eyes. This is to be the moment a mother cherishes and cannot wait for when they have their boys grow up to be a man of their own and send them off with their bride on their wedding day.

It is all of the little things that are the most important. Kim and I hold a lot back at times because it just makes us mad if you we dwell on all of the things we will miss out on with Nathaniel, we could go mad.

We try so hard to function as a normal family, but it is always in the back of your mind, that question, why him? We could be out and enjoying a mom and dad date or we can be out as a whole family, everything going on as normal as can be and I can see a little boy who is the same age as Nathaniel or who looks like Nathaniel and I start to cry. I think of whom we are missing. And the worst of them all is when I come across a child, especially a boy, who has Cerebral Palsy and reminds me of the Nathaniel I know and love. This also reminds me we are not the only ones in this world with these problems. We are a fraternity, as much as we do not want to belong, we strive for our best outcome and then we reach a little further.

My biggest pet-peeve in life is us. Not us as in family, us as in America. Us as in our health care system. I never thought I would have to use the "system" like I am now. What a racket. A universal health care system is mandatory in this country, and I mean right now. It is downright frustrating to have my son turned down for a "pre-existing condition" or you get the "Family Plan" coverage, which you have to pay an arm or a leg for it. And if you are unable to pay when you fall behind in your astronomical bills, I do believe, and it would not surprise me, that they would take an arm or a leg for payment. What I want is to walk into a doctor's office or a hospital, have any test done for Nathaniel that is needed, not to wait for a referral, and walk out with the precise answers needed to help him survive day to day. And not get a bill in the mail that looks like a shopping list with commas on the total. Or have a state entity standing first in line, with a hand out, when they here hear you are getting some type of settlement or trust coming in the near future. What ever happened to bedside manner? What ever happened to house calls? A universal healthcare system is needed in this country now! I would pay a little more a year if I could get whatever we need, in a timely manner. Appointments without referrals, blood work, test. Don't give us "it is too hard to set up and it would take forever." Bullshit! England did it while at war (in their own country) against the German's. And let's not forget, they did not have the technology we have today when they did it, so don't give me your well-rehearsed answers. You will not do it because you are so far into the pharmaceutical company's pockets you cannot find your way out. Quite frankly, I do not think you could find your way out of a brown paper bag, but that is another story for another day.

Third world countries are laughing at us. Are you not embarrassed by this? Your fellow Americans are slipping through your fingers every day. If you think about it long and hard and think back, let's say twenty-five25 years, or at least a generation of doctors ago, what do you think it meant to them to become a doctor? It was pride. Now it is about money and self-thought. The almighty dollar. This is not-so-mighty any more. But this generation, with the exception of a few honest ones, look at it if they do not have the fancy, overpriced cars or two or three luxury homes, they try to streamline more patients through with thoughtless recklessness to be paid more. You are also the ones who are ruining sports for me. You definitely know who you are, Mr. Doctor and Mr. Lawyer. You are the reason why I cannot afford a seat on the first level of my favorite sporting event. These seats are built for you in mind. The person, (I cannot call you a fan) who shows up by the end of the first quarter or period and gets out by the beginning of the last quarter or period. You are too good to walk in with us regular folk and haves to get out before us regular folk, sometimes 55,000 strong, walk past one of his or her luxury cars in that V.I.P. parking lot. Come on, we all see it. It is a damn shame. We have to get our values back. Our dignity. We have to get with the program right now. I know other countries look to us for help to feed kids or get the proper medications to people off the beaten paths, but you are losing at home. It all starts here. Get off your ass and out of others pockets and do something dignified for once. If I hear the word Get the move on for a universal health care system and fix our economy. It will make all of us stronger.

There, I am off my soapbox. Oh wait, this generation does not know what that means, that was last generation of doctors and politicians. A couple of people said to me why go off on a tangent about other things; we should focus on our family and Nathaniel. But I tell them to read it again, what I just wrote impacts us greatly. We cannot afford any of these things. Sporting events to take my son to and enjoy the surroundings, especially the crowd noise. And the most important thing, healthcare, who can afford it? Our world around us affects what we can and cannot do with Nathaniel. We were a middle-class family at one point but not now, we are going lower as we speak. Yes, we can afford to buy a house now, but it is because of Nathaniel's injuries. This house, when we select it, will be for the welfare of Nathaniel. He needs it. He deserves it. He is missing out on life and all of its pleasures.

He will not miss out on love; we have plenty of that to give and then some. But love will only take us so far. Someday, which I hope is later rather than sooner, Nathaniel will not be able to overcome an illness and pass on to heaven, just as we all will do. As much as I will prepare myself for that day, when it arrives I will be a wreck. This heartbreak will totally overpower every situation we went through in his fumbled life. All of that what could have been will come rushing back and flood my mind. The good, the bad, the heartwarming and heartbreaking moments. But I do know Nathaniel will be in a way better place. God has a nice house up there and I know Nathaniel will have his own wing on that house decorated any way he wants it. He will meet all of the people I have talked to him about on those nights we did not have nursing help and I climbed in his bed with him.

I cannot wait until he meets my cousin Anna. In Anna's lifetime, she helped take care of at least sixty 60 kids at one time or another. She helped to mold me into the man I am today along with my mom, Aunt Pat and my grand mom. She will be the perfect one to take care of Nathaniel until Kim and I meet up with him.

When I jump in bed with him, I tell him what I want to talk to him about when we meet in heaven. I want to know if he understood us on earth or did he really feel our love. This is what will make our lives worth living, for that first moment we meet as father and son in heaven. We will talk forever, I know it. I cannot wait to hear his voice. He listens to me every day on earth, so he can bend my ear forever and talk about whatever he wants. Yes, as you can see, I do believe there is a heaven. Listen, I have had so many problems dealing with Nathaniel's life. I lost myself in my hate and rage for long periods of time, I still do at times. Not as bad as before, but it still follows me. Sometimes I am ashamed of it; sometimes I am so damn proud of it. It shows my passion and it has made me get up off my ass and do something with my life, like write this book. I have bottled up my feelings for so long, now I feel some relief. A lot has come out, there was good and bad, but it was necessary. Look at Nathaniel; he has no voice to speak his mind. He needs us to speak up for him. I call it, "For what he can't, we do!"

We are the perfect parents for Nathaniel. We can juggle our lives around the instability of Nathaniel's life and keep up with the young lives of Courtney and Emma. Kim and I have the knack of doing everything the way it needs to be done in a timely manner and correctly. No matter how tiring it may be, we have never looked at one another and said something to the effect of "I quit" or "I cannot do this anymore."

Recently, we were going through some pictures and video of all of us, especially Nathaniel, from his birth up until 2006. As I looked at every picture, I remembered what I was feeling at that very moment. It all came rushing back to me. The videos have that damn beeping from the N.I.C.U. monitors that makes me cringe as if someone just pulled their fingernails across a chalkboard. And of course, Nathaniel's crying. The consistent wail of an infant was deafening to one's ear and one's soul. He was new to our world and it seemed he was so scared or in constant pain. "How long can we go on like this?" Kim and I would ask each other. I remember one night I was walking around our living room and dining room in our house in Drexel Hill, PA carrying Nathaniel, who was crying, of course. I remember telling him, "listen, it is 4:10 AM and we need to go to sleep if you can stop crying and relax." As I continue to walk, he settled down in my arms and was looking in my direction. We didn't know he could not see at this time, but I felt him listening to me talk. The silence may have lasted 10 minutes or so when Nathaniel started to cry again. I started to have a feeling at that moment our lives were going to be total chaos. I had the sense of helplessness. No matter what I did, I had no control. At times, even today, we still have no control, but we have been down that road and back about a thousand times and we deal. We cannot fix the past and I would love to put the past as far away from my mind as possible, but we need it there for Courtney and Emma's future. Everyone's past is so important to one's psyche. Who wouldn't want to remember your own times growing up? I keep telling Courtney already that I want her to enjoy every moment of childhood. She was thrusted into a world of unrest at the age of 2 and has had to put up with a lot of shit for a thirteen 13-year-old. Kim and I are constantly watching the girls and making sure there is no ill will towards Nathaniel or they start to have trouble with the handling everyday activities. We have the support and the outlets in place if they start to have trouble with anything. I do not want the stress that Kim and I deal with affect them. They have seen things other kids their age may never see. They know Nathaniel is sick and

I guess they expect things may happen to him so they just go on with their lives and go with the flow. Sometimes under protest, like when they are scheduled to go somewhere or do something with their friends, but they go along with what is happening. For the hand that was dealt to us, I do believe that Kim and I are good parents. We always try to keep a simple plan. One, Nathaniel has to be comfortable and as healthy as possible. Two, Courtney and Emma need to be happy. They need the separation from Nathaniel so they can walk in their own shoes and become bright young girls. I know they love him and miss what he could have been with him being a health boy. Third, my beautiful wife Kimberly, the woman I love, the woman I cherish. She goes through so much on her own and then she handles everything associated with Nathaniel. If we can get her well with her Crohn's, even if we can cut down on the number of flare-ups per year, I know Kim would feel so much better for longer periods of time. I fear for Kim and Nathaniel. Nathaniel has irreversible damage to his brain and Kim lives with a disease with no cure. There is hope for Kim, it sounds like we are close to a medicine that may almost put Crohn's into remission. There is even talk about small intestine transplant surgery in the world. I need to keep Kim well. Right now, I can only imagine how she would feel with no active Crohn's.

There is a path carved out for each of us in this world and I think I have found mine. My legal notes turned into feelings. Very, very raw feelings. I have to let go of my built up sorrow and rage, even the disgust towards my fellow man and I must try to find the higher road. I think I am doing it. I want people to know my son because he deserves only the best. He cannot get it for himself, so Kim and I have to provide for him. Forever. Forever is long time, but it has to be done. You know, during our legal action that we took one lawyer suggested, in my presence, that the best way to cut down on cost in any case like this is to place the child in a home. A very sneaky, backhanded remark, which struck a nerve in my damaged soul. I thought, "Put yourself in my shoes for one day, just one day, and look into my son's eyes and tell him I cannot do this anymore and we have to put you in a home." The child may not understand, but it would tear you to pieces. It hurts me to think of Nathaniel with us not around. How scared would he be? His association with us is by voice and by sounds, he knows who we are as soon as we open our mouths, and if that is not "there for him" then I have not done my job in life or I have not taken good enough care of myself to be there for him. It really scares me to death to think this way, but it is in my mind and I constantly have to push myself to be better for my family and myself. I am ready to tackle the future, and going through the last 11 years has made us more prepared to accept whatever is thrown our way.

The other thing I worry about is being selfish. I want Nathaniel to be here a long, long time but there will come a day when Kim and I will have to make a decision or a series of decisions of when is "enough is enough.". We struggle with this every day. Look at Nathaniel's scoliosis, it is not going to get any better and we have decided no surgery. I cannot put him through the pain of this surgery and the repeat surgeries needed as he grows down the road. Forget it! The other decision, which is the hardest Kim and I have made in our lives, is to sign a Do Not Resuscitate Medical Care Order, which is no CPR if arrest occurs. Now, before you go off the handle, it is an order to give maximum effort to prevent cardiac arrest. Why do this, you may ask? If Nathaniel has a seizure that sets him into cardiac arrest, or if he develops pneumonia to the point he must be resuscitated and/ or put on a ventilator to breathe, he will lose more oxygen to his already damaged brain and the outcome will be more devastating to an already devastated life. The Nathaniel we have now will be the best we will ever have him. He unfortunately can only get worse. He practically would be brain dead. There is no reversal of fortunes here. Do I believe in miracles? Yes. Do I believe in reality? Yes, more than miracles. Now I know some people are out there saying, "How could you?" I am saying the same thing. How could I? But we just know. I do not know how I know, we just deal. I have to take my selfishness out of the equation and live with our decision in life and believe they are for the best for everyone involved. It does not show we are giving up or that we are quitters. Do you think the decision was an easy one? Hell no! Do I feel we are cheating Nathaniel out of his life? What life! His life was stolen at birth. Remember in the dedication in the front of this book. I wrote "For my son Nathaniel, whose life has not turned out the way he wanted it to be." He was ready for this world and it was ripped from his grasp. He loves the attention he gets, but don't you think he rather be running around playing, getting dirty and driving his sisters crazy. He was cheated. It was no act of God, it was no damage caused four or five days prior to his birth. Look into my son's eyes and tell him you are sorry for what happened, do not tell us. I am tired of hearing it. He deserves the well wishes and prayers. Give him the praise for trying his best through life and he does not even know he is doing it. He can teach us all a lesson in life. To the edge of life and back several times and doing it with brain damage, poor immune system, some sort of blindness, no motor skills. I am truly humbled by my little buddy. I dare not catch myself complain about a slight cold ever again.

So who am I? I am just a dad! A dad who has been given a challenge of a lifetime. To raise two beautiful and well girls and a disabled son. I am a husband! A husband who has a wife who embodies the words soul mate and she holds every characteristic in the meaning of motherhood. Also, I am lucky! I am lucky God has not struck me down where I stand. I have said some hateful things since Nathaniel was born and I have repented and pleaded for forgiveness of my sins many times. But if I start wandering around in my mind, come across an item, or picture from Nathaniel's birth, I do revert back to my lost ways. I cannot help it. All of this is so unnecessary and it has caused ill will. I do not know if I can totally forgive in my lifetime. The saying time heals old wounds could come across my mind someday, but I can tell you it will not be any time soon. My family has been screwed over through this whole mess. I worry about Kim's illness. She has not been feeling good for almost a year now. Her stomach hurts 24/7 and sometimes nobody knows what to do for her or they do not believe she is in that much pain at times.

After a long 7-year battle with our nation's legal system, our time was finally over with our matters of the heart and their matters of who cares. This has truly left a sour taste in our mouths. Kim and I look at each other and wonder if we did the right thing. There is not much there if Nathaniel sticks it out for the long haul.

There was a trust set up for Nathaniel and not much will go in it. After everyone involved (lawyers, creditors and state entities) had their hands out and got paid, there was a little left over that was going to be put back into the trust that was set up for Nathaniel. So Kim and I started to wonder if we could use this money to buy a house with what was left over. Of course, this is not easy to do. The first step is to ask the judge to meet with us and if he gives us the OK for the meeting, we must go and plead our case. Our case was heard and we are allowed to move forward and find a house we can call our own. Then come to find out as I am meeting with the judge, back at home in Frederick, Kim was admitted to the hospital that morning. She told everyone not to tell me so I would stay and talk with the judge. This is just so typical for us Breen's, never a dull moment around here. Without this decision from the judge we could never be able to buy a house. So our search was lengthy, about 6 months, but we have found our house. It is more than what was given to us by the judge but we did qualify for a mortgage somehow. The housing market sucks so badly, they are handing out mortgages like candy with low rates, so we made out well. I don't know how, and I am not going to ask how. I am just going to shut up. Our mortgage payment will be less than our rent payment, and guess what, we own. What? Let me say it again, we own! Kim and I keep looking at each other and keep saying, "Is this really happening?" The way we look at it is that Nathaniel has a place to call home. He will have his own master suite on the first floor and a bathroom that is bigger than his bedroom-dining room he was living in our old townhouse we were renting. This is all for Nathaniel and the girls. No more moving every two years, no more paying out money for something we did not own. Yes, there are still the medical bills and they keep mounting, but maybe we can overcome some of the things that stress us out in the first place.

(January 17, 2008)

(Today, after a month, which started with come and go pain in her belly, has become one steady pain. Kim has to have another CAT-scan, which showed what they thought was the return of her Crohn's Disease just as bad as it was before her last surgery three months ago. She had a CAT-scan as soon as the pain started a month ago and the doctors said it showed nothing. She is in a tremendous amount of constant pain, but once again, no one believes how much pain she really is in. She called me at work in tears. She has never called me in tears. Tears because she is right back where she started from three months ago and no one believed her until today. And who knows what these doctors are seeing. How could she have the Crohn's as bad as before the last surgery? Something is not right here. This sucks! Again!)

The whole time we were planning to buy and move to our house, Kim was really having a tough time with her disease. She was in and out of the hospital and our nerves were shot and Kim was at her breaking point and just wanted to get better but no one was coming up with the answer for her problems. She finally had to have surgery, which everyone was trying to avoid and use this as a last ditch effort but the medicines were not working. Kim usually gets better for a good while and the Crohn's subsides, but this time things were different. She kept feeling something pulling in her stomach. Kim knew there was something wrong because after her previous surgeries she was mostly pain free. She goes back to her gastro doctor and he says since she had her third surgery in the same area over a couple of years, her muscles are contracting and it will take a longer period to heal.

She sees another gastro doctor and after a few so-called tests, he determines her Crohn's is the same as before the surgery. Again, no one really knows what is going on but this is only the beginning or the proverbial tip of the iceberg. In and out of the hospital again, but this time in Baltimore. It was finally determined she had an abscess around her last resection. Medicine was given for a while to treat it but that was not working. Another surgery was done to remove the abscess. OK? Not yet. Five days later Kim was rushed back into surgery because she ruptured. For the second time in my life, I was scared for someone else's life rather than my own. Kim is so strong from the inside out but this past year has made her depressed and she feels like she is becoming less of a mother and wife to the kids and me. I never saw her like this before and don't want to see it again. I really had to build her up again and not let her feel down. We need her so, so bad. I cannot imagine our lives without her, she needs to heal and conquer this disease. There is no cure for Crohn's, but right now, we have put it into remission, Kim can go on with her life a little easier. Fourteen hospital stays of four days or more over a 13 month period, the last one over a month, would rattle the best of us. I hope it's over for a long time and maybe a cure will be found soon or at least a medicine that can manage one's life. And then there was the whole moving into our new house project that Kim missed out on. I tell her all the time, if she just wanted to not pack up and move, she did not have to go through all of this hospital and surgery stuff. I get one of those looks that a wife gives her husband when he is talking out of his ass. Guys, you know what I mean; we have all seen this look. Well, I hope we will be in remission for a long time and we can go on as normal as possible.

Then there is yours truly, Chris Breen, father of Nathaniel Breen. I really do not know if my wounds will ever heal. I am a somewhat shattered father. My boy was taken from me at his birth. We live in an upside down world around our house. Just when we think things are good, another thing goes haywire. It could be something new or something old that pops up again. I try to handle things without banging my head on the wall. There are times I am cynical, Kim helps me see the way, and I do it for her also. When I say something cynical, I hate myself. I know that is not me. When I am on my game, I am proud, a proud father of three kids. But there is a special spot for Nathaniel, who has broadened my mind to things I never thought I had to deal with. Nathaniel shows me courage. I do not know to what capacity he knows his dad, but he leads me to the true meaning of the word love. Love has a new dimension in my life. It is stronger than everything I have ever felt before and at times, I do not know if I should cry or laugh because of that love. Maybe I have cried too many tears in anger and I might do it again but I must regroup from that and live this love.

One of my biggest hurdles I had to overcome was my own bitterness. My outer circumstances have been changing the quality of my life and its surroundings. All of us want to have the highest quality of life possible but behind all of my anger, rage and sadness there is the sense that things should be a certain way and Nathaniel did not receive his entitled life because of the trust of other people was not there.

Growing up I was told in God's world, or heaven as people know it, we are taught all of your pain and suffering is gone. My problem is we are in the world as it is today, or we are not in the world of what should have been. This is the very spot my bitterness comes from. As I relate to this, I am trying to identify where I can let the bad emotions go. Through the book I have relived the bad things that have happened to Nathaniel and things he cannot do and it shoots my level of anger up in intensity but there is no way to satisfy the anger and it just hangs around in my mind with nowhere to go. It has changed me. I have become a cynical person, sometimes to the point I did not want to see other people happy. A lower grade of hostility sets in also. I have lived with it since Nathaniel's birth and at times I didn't even notice it was still there, it became a façade to me.

Is it time for me to be real? The struggle in my soul has consumed me. When I questioned mom if God was really there, I truly meant it. I lost every portion of my faith. Where and when do I come out of this funk? Do I just learn to accept the damage already done and move on? I still want my answers. I want personal apologies. I want someone to look me in the eyes and say they made a mistake. Then I step back and I see myself saying "I want this!" and "I want that!" this is where the bitterness builds, and it is dangerous. If I don't find a way to control it could become turbulent and ruin everything I have. Health, friendships, even marriage. Man, it could become my own little prison for my soul.

I have to find my way back to know that faith, forgiveness and love are more powerful. Once this happens maybe I can see God is really calling out to me and that he has been there the whole time and is guiding me somehow. The struggles of life will never stop, it is how we manage and recover from them makes us who we are. Will I get there? Who knows? Will I try harder? Yes. I must learn to cope with Nathaniel's injuries and accept all of the troubles he goes through. I am his dad and he needs me. I am ready for the future and whatever it has to throw at me. Dad's, I would ask you to walk a mile in my shoes and see the path I am following. It is one of the most winding paths you will find but I want you to stick to yours and do what is right for yourself and your kids. Please do not give up. It all begins at home with you and your significant other by giving them your honest love. Make the time by striving to be your best.

I feel the weights are beginning to come off my shoulders. I really feel it, I hope this trend continues. Kim and I make sure we are motivated to tackle any obstacle that comes our way. But there are certain words that will always be in the back of my mind; No matter how much effort we put into our lives, we will not function as a normal family. I now can deal with that. If we make the hardest of tasks work to a certain degree and if Kim, Courtney, Nathaniel, Emma and I are somewhat healthy, happy and comfortable, my soul is happy.

I thank you for letting me bend your ear for a while. Nathaniel's story had to be told and I thought what better way to do it than in my own written words from an old copybooks and a black leather journal. Could not put it on a computer, cannot afford one. But I hope my words did not offend you but I hope they struck a chord in your heart. The families in this world with these similar problems need to be heard and need to be looked after. I hope these words will help another father stand up, take charge of their families, and become an active figure in the lives of their children. Disabled or not. They need our guidance. And to Nathaniel, my Son, daddy is here for you. You are my life and you inspire me to become a better man and father. I am your advocate in life and together we will walk forever. I Love You, Daddy!

Edited by: Lori Rypka